The PESTLE, The CAGE & The SMART Models:

Business Analysis Tools

To Learn & Apply to Your Business

By
Abdelali BOUZID

Copyright © 2020 Abdelali Bouzid

All rights reserved.

ASIN: .xxxxxxxxxxxxx

Abdelali BOUZID

Accessible at Website:

www.ab-consulting-online.com

Or Via

My Author Page:

http://amzn.to/1U2qePT

An Online Course accompanying this book is accesible here: *http://ab-consulting-online.com/ur-online-courses/*.
Other books and Related Courses on Business Analysis topics are also published to help you develop your skills and know-how on the matter, check them here:

http://ab-consulting-online.com/my-kindle-books/

WHAT'S THIS BOOK ABOUT:

The Book is organised in two main Sections both focusing on Business Analysis. The first Section does so through the PESTLE Model and the second concentrates on the CAGE Analysis Framework.

WHAT'S THE 'PESTLE' SECTION (I) ABOUT:

This section is to provide you with an insight into Business Analysis through a powerful Analytical Tool, the PESTLE Framework, which is commonly used by Business Analysts, Consultants, and Managers.

The Section is organized in line with the six Perspectives of the PESTLE Business Model, for clarity. For practicality, it introduces each of these six Dimensions in some details through examples and case studies, and apply them to real-life situations. This will empower the Reader, to develop the concepts learnt into practical skills: practice what he has learnt.

I wrote this Section so as to enable you to develop your understanding of Business Analysis (BA) Tools, and empower such learning through practice, by applying the PESTLE Framework, as a powerful BA Tool, to concrete case studies and by means of interactive exercises.

The Section addresses each of these six entities (Political, Economic, Social, Technological, Legal, Environmnetal) in some details and adopts a rigorous method to alleviate the technical complexities involved.

Altogether the Section provides you with a basic guide to Business analysis through a powerful yet manageable Business Analysis Tool. Different examples and Case-Studies are used to simplify the complex aspects of the model in a practical environment. The hands-on approach used will help you in this process.

Finally the Section is intended to help you develop your problem solving skills and your decision making capacity and adds another Dimension the CAGE Framework of SECTION (II).

WHAT'S THE 'CAGE' SECTION (II) ABOUT:

This section is to provide you with an insight into Business Analysis through some a powerful Analytical Tool, the CAGE Framework, which is commonly used by Business Analysts, Consultants, and Managers.

The Section was written to introduce each of the four Perspectives of the CAGE Model. It addresses each of these Dimensions in some details through examples and case studies, including their areas of application, as appropriate.

It then moves on to address the four Dimensions together, to derive a Global Analysis view, a helicopter view.

Finally, the Section was written to empower the Reader, to develop the skills learnt through a hands-on session, through a Business analysis Project whereby he is given the opportunity to practice what he has learnt.

I wrote this Section so as to enable you to develop your understanding of Business Analysis (BA) Tools, and empower such learning through practice, by applying the CAGE Framework, as a powerful BA Tool, to concrete case studies and by means of interactive exercises.

It was writen to add another Dimension to the PESTLE Framework of SECTION (I).

WHAT'S THE 'SMART' SECTION (III) ABOUT:

The section is about Learning and Applying the SMART Objectives: Specifiable, Measurable, Accessible, Realistic, Time-Bound.

Learn and Apply the S.M.A.R.T Model to your Business Objectives; SMART spelling five acronyms: Specifiable, Measurable, Accessible, Realistic, Time-Bound. The Section will shine light through the Model and its 5 perspectives through concrete examples and scenarios which enable the learner to put the model into practice and in a real life context. This develops the power of problem solving, decision making and rigor in the business analysis.

Your success will be attributed to assessing your business (or that of your client) from different perspectives and lead you to making decisions quickly, objectively, effectively and efficiently in a logical, structured manner: you will be taught here the **SMART Business Analysis** tool to do just that!

The **SMART** model which you will learn in this section is a **Strategic Tool that is often used by Professionals such as Consultants and Analysts -** who are welcome to join the Course to consolidate their skills. However, the step-by-step approach adopted here makes the Course accessible to ALL and easy to use by EACH and everyone.

Will benefit strongly from the section, those who wish to develop an objective approach to Business Analysis, Problem Solving and Decision Making

You need to complete all the lectures to develop the inherent SMART Skills. But, you do not need any prior knowledge of this SMART Analysis model.

Reach over Now, click the button and "Join in the Learning". You will master this powerful Business Analysis Model, its Framework and its application as a Tool which harnesses fundamental skills that will accompany you for life: a first class investment, no doubt!

An Online Course accompanying this book is accesible here: *http://ab-consulting-online.com/ur-online-courses/*.

Other books and Related Courses on Business Analysis topics are also published to help you develop your skills and know-how on the matter, check them here: *http://ab-consulting-online.com/my-kindle-books/*

AUTHOR PROFILE

Abdelali BOUZID is a trilingual Consultant - Coach, Author, Infopreneur & Online Instructor in different sectors including Management, Training, Computing, Business Quality, Business Analysis, Technology, etc. : 25+ years experience through a wide and diverse Career developed in United Kingdom and extended to North Africa.

After graduating as an Airline Pilot (with CPL & ATPL) from Oxford Aviation Academy, Oxford - UK, he moved on to Computer Sciences where he Post-Graduated (with an MSc - Computer sciences) from Brunel University, London.

As Consultancy - Coaching and Management Training dominated his business activities he went on for Post-Graduation in Management / Business Administration and earned an MBA from the University of Wales (UK).

" Today's dream is for me to share with you - wherever you are - my life's treasure, this modest wealth of Experience, Knowledge and Professional Know-How through Writing, Publishing, Seminars, On-line Teaching and Communicating "-

Abdelali

LINKS TO THE AUTHOR @ SOCIAL & PROFESSIONAL PLATFORMS

You may reach me here:

Linkedin: *https://www.linkedin.com/in/abdelali-bouzid-39091823/*

Twitter: *https://www.twitter.com/@sonsalab*

Facebook: *https://www.facebook.com/abdelali.bouzid.3*

My Author Page: *http://amzn.to/1U2qePT*

A WHOLE SERIES OF EBOOKS AND THEIR ACCOMPANYING ONLINE COURSES HAVE BEEN PUBLISHED BY THE AUTHOR TO OFFER THE FOLLOWER A COMPREHENSIVE BUSINESS ANALYSIS JOURNEY FROM DIFFERENT PERSPECTIVES,

Check them out here:

1- *http://ab-consulting-online.com/ur-kindle-books/*
2- *http://ab-consulting-online.com/ur-online-courses/*

The On-Line Course accompanying this Book is accessible here:

http://ab-consulting-online.com/ur-online-courses/

Abdelali BOUZID

OTHER BOOKS BY THE AUTHOR

http://amzn.to/1U2qePT

'Organizational Behavior: Business Analysis through a Case Study', **Available at:** *http://amzn.to/1V08IuL*	
'Marketing Management: Business Analysis and Planning from a Marketing Perspective' **Available At:** *http://Amzn.To/1w1ckyd*	
'International Business Management Analysis: Strategy, Partnership, Investment, Benefits &Global Brands and Supply Chain. **Available At:** *http://amzn.to/1LGHiaO*	
Learn & Apply Business Analysis Tools: 7s Framework, Swot And Balanced Scorecard: to Assess a Small Business - Print & Kindle **Available At:** *https://www.amazon.co.uk/dp/B072N9PSWG*	
'Applying Business Analysis Tools: To Assess A Small Business', **Available At:** *http://Amzn.To/1m9cbpx*	
'The 7s Model & The Cage Framework: Business Analysis Tools' **Available at:** *https://www.amazon.co.uk/dp/B085T8SXP4*	
'The Pestle Business Analysis Tool: To Learn & Apply To Your Business' **Available At:** *https://www.amazon.co.uk/dp/B085RB329Z*	

'Business Analysis Tools: The CAGE Framework Applied Available at: https://www.amazon.co.uk/dp/B085MN1QHV	
'Business Analysis Tools: The Multi-Criteria analysis: To Study Your Business Available At: https://www.amazon.co.uk/dp/B085NBNLYF	
Business Analysis Tool-Kit & its Application: 7S Framework, SWOT & Balanced Scorecard Available At: https://www.amazon.co.uk/dp/B084KNRXRVWG	
Learn & Apply Business Analysis Tools: 7s Framework, Swot And Balanced Scorecard: to Assess a Small Business - Print & Kindle Available At: https://www.amazon.co.uk/dp/B072N9PSWG	

ONLINE COURSES BY THE AUTHOR ON THE SUBJECT

The Courses below complement and empower the Topic of this Book, *"Business Analysis & Tools"*, if you enjoy quality digital content, audio and interactive online courses led by a Professional Instructor.

Over 4900 Students from about 110 Countries follow these Courses; If you want to join them:
http://ab-consulting-online.com/ur-online-courses/

Course-1:
Problem Solving & Decision Making: Tools, Techniques &Method":

{http://ab-consulting-online.com/ur-online-courses/}

Course-2
Business Analysis Tools: Apply SMART, PESTLE, CAGE, 7S, Porter's-5Forces

{http://ab-consulting-online.com/ur-online-courses/}

Course-3
Learn & Apply the Multi-Criteria Business Analysis Tool

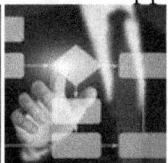

{http://ab-consulting-online.com/ur-online-courses/}

Course-4
Learn & Apply the Business Analysis Tools: 7S & CAGE

{http://ab-consulting-online.com/ur-online-courses/}

Course-5
Learn & Apply the CAGE - Business Analysis Tool

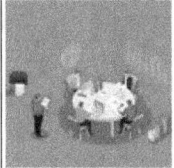

{http://ab-consulting-online.com/ur-online-courses/}

Course-6
Learn & Apply the S.M.A.R.T Model to Business Objectives

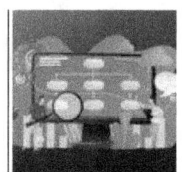

{http://ab-consulting-online.com/ur-online-courses/}

Course-7
Learn & Apply the P.E.S.T.L.E Business Analysis Tool

{http://ab-consulting-online.com/ur-online-courses/}

A NOTE FROM THE AUTHOR

Thank you very much for taking the time to read:

" The PESTLE Model & The CAGE Framework: Business Analysis Tools"

If you find it interesting please take a moment to leave a review at your online convenient retailer such as Amazon UK or Amazon USA.

As an appreciated reader, you are most welcome to contact me via my website {*http://www.ab-consulting-online.com*} where you can sign up for my newsletter to be notified of new releases, editions, and to benefit from my blog.

You may join me / connect with me on the different social networking platforms shown above: Linkedin, Facebook. Twiter, etc..

Abdelali BOUZID

CONTENTS

What's This Book About: iv
What's The 'PESTLE' Section (I) About: iv
What's The 'CAGE' Section (II) About: v
What's The 'SMART' Section (III) About: vi
Author Profile ix
Links to the Author @ Social & Professional Platforms x
Other BOOKS By The Author xi
Online COURSES By The Author On The Subject xiii
A Note From The Author 1
CONTENTS 3
FIGURES & TABLES 6
Figures: 7
Tables: 9
Executive Summary 11

SECTION I 16
Learn & Apply 'The PESTLE Business Analysis Model' .. 16
Introduction 18
1. PESTEL-Analysis, Perspective 20
2. The PESTLE Analysis - Political 24
3. The PESTLE Analysis – Economic 26
4. The PESTLE Analysis – Social 28
5. The PESTLE Analysis - Technical/technological 30
6. The PESTLE Analysis – Legal 31
7. The PESTLE Analysis – Environmental 33
8. PESTLE-Analysis, Implementation Issues & Opportunities 35
9. Applying PESTLE Analysis-1 43

10. Applying PESTLE Analysis-2 50
11. PRACTICE: PESTLE-Architecture & Case Study 60
12. Conclusion of the Section 77
ANNEX-A: 80
'PESTLE' Analysis applied to Algeria E-Commerce 80

SECTION II 83
Business Analysis Tools Applied: 'THE CAGE Framework' 83
Executive Summary: THE 'CAGE' 84
The CAGE - Introduction 87
1. The CAGE - Cultural Dimension 92
2. The CAGE - Administrative Dimension 96
3. The CAGE - Geographic Dimension 100
4. The CAGE - Economic Dimension 105
5. The CAGE - From All Four Perspectives 110
6. The CAGE- PROJECT (Practice) 117
ANNEX - A: Resources (The CAGE) 125
Bibliography (The CAGE) 134

SECTION III 136
"Learn and Apply The 'SMART' Goals Model " 136
THE 'SMART Model' - Introduction 137
1. SMART Objectives - What are they? 138
2. SMART Objectives - What for? 141
3. SMART Key Elements - "Specific" 144
4. SMART Key Elements - "Measurable" 146
5. SMART Key Elements - "Attainable" 149
6. SMART Key Elements - "Realistic" 151

7. SMART Key Elements - "Time-Bound" 153
8. SMART Objectives - 156
"Scenarios / Examples" 156
9. SMART Objectives - Conclusion 162
10. SMART Objectives - Psycholog: The Yale Story 166
11. SMART Objectives - PROJECT: Hands-On Practice
.... 169
A Note from The Author 172
ONLINE Courses By The Author On The Subject 174
Other BOOKS By The Author 177

FIGURES & TABLES

FIGURES:

SECTION-I [PESTLE]
Figure.1: The PESTLE Analysis, Perspective 20
Figure.2: The PESTLE Analysis, the 'Political' aspect...................24
Figure.3: The PESTLE Analysis, the 'Economic' aspect...............26
Figure.4: The PESTLE Analysis, the 'social' aspect 28
Figure.5: The PESTLE Analysis, the 'technological' aspect..........30
Figure.6: The PESTLE Analysis, the 'legal' aspect 31
Figure.7: The PESTLE Analysis, the 'environmental' aspect........33
Figure.8: The PESTLE Analysis, Implementation issues...............35
Figure.9: Applying the PESTLE Analysis1 43
Figure.10: Applying the PESTLE Analysis2.....................50
Figure.11: Applying the PESTLE Analysis2, Stages.......................51
Figure.12: Applying the PESTLE Analysis2, Procedure 52
Figure.13: PESTLE Analysis2, Procedure - Brainstorming...........54
Figure.14: PESTLE Analysis2, Procedure - Vote Brainstorming .55
Figure.15: PESTLE Analysis2, 'Impact Rating'.................56
Figure.16: PESTLE Analysis2, 'Weighted Vote' 57
Figure.17: PESTLE Analysis2, 'Plan of Action'.....................58
Figure.19: PESTLE Analysis2, 'Case Study-1: Algeria' 60
Figure.20: PESTLE Analysis2, Conclusion 77

SECTION-II [CAGE]
Figure.1: The CAGE, Introduction 87
Figure.2: The CAGE Introduction, Model Representation 88
Figure.2a: The CAGE Introduction, DeBeers Example 89
Figure.2b: The CAGE, DeBeers - Administrative Dimension......89
Figure.3: The CAGE, Cultural Dimension - Context....................92
Figure.4: The CAGE, DeBeers - Cultural Dimension 93
Figure.5: The CAGE, Administrative Dimension 96
Figure.6: The CAGE, Administrative dimension - study 97
Figure.7: The CAGE, Geographic Dimension - Context 100
Figure.8: The CAGE, Geographic Dimension -Study.................101
Figure.9: The CAGE, Economic Dimension - Context................105
Figure.10: The CAGE, Economic Dimension - Study.................106
Figure.11: The CAGE, From All Four Dimensions - Context ...110

Figure.12: The CAGE, From All Four Dimensions - Study 111
Figure.13: The CAGE, Project (Practice): 'Cultural Distance'.....117
Figure.14: The CAGE, Project: 'Administrative Distance'..........119
Figure.15: The CAGE, Project: 'Geographic Distance'.................120
Figure.16: The CAGE, Project: 'Economic Distance' 121
Figure.17: The CAGE, Project: 'Global Analysis' 122

SECTION-III {SMART]
Figure.1: S.M.A.R.T Objectives: What Are They?.........................138
Figure.2: S.M.A.R.T Goals, Key Elements 139
Figure.3: S.M.A.R.T Goals, the Model 140
Figure.4: S.M.A.R.T Key Elements: Specifiable..............................144
Figure.5: S.M.A.R.T Key Elements: Measurable.............................146
Figure.6: S.M.A.R.T Goals, Triangulation 148
Figure.7: S.M.A.R.T Key Elements: Accessible / Attainable........149
Figure.8: S.M.A.R.T Key Elements: Realistic 151
Figure.9: S.M.A.R.T Key Elements: Time-Bound 153
Figure.10: S.M.A.R.T Key Elements: Scenarios / Examples.......156
Figure.11: S.M.A.R.T Goals: Conclusion 162
Figure.12: S.M.A.R.T Objectives: Key elements...........................163
Figure.13: S.M.A.R.T Objectives: The Model 164
Figure.14: S.M.A.R.T Model: Psychology - Yale University 166
Figure.15: S.M.A.R.T Objectives: Project 169

TABLES:

SECION-I [PESTLE]
Table.1: PESTLE Analysis, 'Case Study-1: Algeria' 62
Table.2: PESTLE Analysis, 'Case Study-1: Algeria, Part.2' 68
Table.3: PESTLE Analysis, 'Case Study-1: Algeria, Part.3' 72
Table.4: Annex-A, PESTLE Analysis 'Global Case Study' 80

SECION-II [CAGE]
Table.1: The CAGE Analysis, Example: DeBeers Case Study......90
Table.2: The CAGE Analysis - Cultural Perspective.......................94
Table.3: The CAGE Analysis - Administrative Perspective...........98
Table.4: The CAGE Analysis - Geographic Perspective..............102
Table.5: The CAGE Analysis - Economic Perspective 107
Table.6: The CAGE Analysis - From All 4 Perspectives (1/2)...112
Table.7: The CAGE Analysis - From All 4 Perspectives (2/2)...114
Table.8: The CAGE, Project (Practice): 'Cultural' Distance' 118
Table.9: The CAGE, Project: *'Administrative' Distance*'...................119
Table.10: The CAGE, Project: *'Geographic' Distance*' 120
Table.11: The CAGE, Project: *'Economic' Distance*'..........................122
Table.12: The CAGE, Project (Practice): *'Global Analysis*'............123

EXECUTIVE SUMMARY

About this Book (PESTLE - CAGE - SMART)

The book is a step by step guide to help you to learn and apply three of the most powerful Business Analysis Tools - the **PESTLE Analysis,** the **CAGE framework** and the **SMART Model**, to analyse and study your business (or that of your client).

The **PESTLE Analysis,** the **CAGE framework** and the **SMART Model,** are acronyms, referring each to a set of specific perspectives from which to assess any Enterprise, as follows:

- The **PESTLE** focuses on: the Political, Economic, Social, Technological, Legal and Environmental aspects,

- The **CAGE** focuses on the perspectives of: Cultural, Administrative, Geographical and Economic, and.

- The **S.M.A.R.T Objectives Model** concentrates on a set of five Key Elements: Specifiable, Measurable, Accessible, Realistic, Time-Bound. Through these elements of the model the reader learns a professional approach to setting up business and personal objectives in a precise, concise and rigorous way. This empowers further your problem solving and decision making capacity.

At first site these three models have different focus and as such complete one another, if used together in the same study.

Your success will be attributed to Analysing your Business (or that of your client) and lead you to making decisions quickly, objectively, effectively and efficiently in a logical, structured manner: you will be taught here the **PESTLE Analysis,** the **CAGE framework** and the **SMART Model**, three Business Analysis Tools which allow you to do just that!

The **PESTLE Analysis,** the **CAGE framework** and the **SMART Model** which you will learn in here, are powerful Tools that are often used by Professionals such as Consultants, **Analysts,** Decision Makers, etc. The step-by-step approach adopted here makes the Book accessible to ALL and easy to use by EACH and everyone.

You need to complete all the key chapters to develop the inherent Business Analysis Skills. But, you do not need any prior knowledge of the **PESTLE,** the **CAGE** and the **SMART** Business Analysis models.

What you'll learn

- You will learn the **PESTLE Analysis,** the **CAGE framework** and the **SMART Model,** three powerful Business Analysis Tools together with their perspectives that can be adapted and adopted to every business case and their appropriate techniques and methods and how these will help you solve problems and make objective decisions.

Are there any requirements or prerequisites?

- The only requirement is to come with an open mind and a drive to learn and apply these powerful Business Analysis Tools to aid business assessment, problem solving and decision making.

Who this book is for:

- Those who will benefit more from this guide are those who want to learn and apply such powerful Business Analysis Tools to aid their business assessment, their Problem Solving and their Decision Making.

Updates to the Book:

Any updates to the book may be announced through my website: *www.ab-consulting-online.com*, together with my Courses related to this book.

To further develop your skills & know-how on BA check my other Books & Online Courses here: *www.ab-consulting-online.com*.

Reach over Now, Click the Button and Join in the Learning!

You will master these powerful Business Analysis & Problem Solving Models, their Frameworks and their application as Tools which harness fundamental skills that will accompany you for life: a first class investment, no doubt!

SECTION I

LEARN & APPLY 'THE PESTLE BUSINESS ANALYSIS MODEL'

Objective:

To Master Architecture, Perspective and Application of the PESTLE Dimensions: Political, Economic, Social, Technological, Legal and Environmental.

INTRODUCTION

This section is a practical and a step by step guide to understanding and implementing the PESTLE Business Analysis tool to assess your Business and develop your Problem Solving skills and Decision Making capacity.

The section provides you with the essential information and the approach to assess your business, solve its problems and tackle difficult decisions you have to take; all of which would save you a great deal of time.

It offers you a golden opportunity to learn what analytic tools are. It helps you to carry out Business Analysis on your own organisation (or that of your Client) and to assess it effectively. It teaches you the method, the structure, and the tool of the PESTLE Analysis model, together with its perspectives

The section will lead you to apply the six Perspectives within the PESTLE Analysis (Political, Economic, Social, Technological, Legal, Environmnetal). It does so through concrete examples and appropriate case studies. and prepares you for application of these in real life-situations within your business.

As an Entrepreneur, a Manager, a CEO, a Small Business Owner, an Analyst, a Freelancer, a Consultant you will develop the basis of Problem Solving and Decision Making through the application of the PESTLE model and its associated perspectives.

This section will help you digest and apply the material presented through illustrative Case Studies and concrete examples. It will teach you the method and approach as well as the tool to carry out Business Analysis (BA) on your own enterprise (or that of your client).

Success is often attributed to Solving Problems in business and Making Decisions quickly, objectively, effectively and efficiently in a logical, structured manner: the PESTLE Analysis tool intends to do just.

The step-by-step approach adopted here makes the learning process accessible to ALL and easy to learn and apply by EACH and everyone. Although you do not need any prior knowledge of this PESTLE Analysis model, you need to complete all the chapters herein to develop the inherent Problem Solving Skills and Decision Making capacity. The only requirement is to come with an open mind and a drive to learn and apply this powerful analysis tool.

If you follow these guidelines, you will master the Business Analysis model and its inherent Decision Making & Problem Solving Model processes, its Framework and its Application as a Tool which harnesses fundamental skills that will accompany you for life: a first class investment, no doubt!

1. PESTEL-ANALYSIS, PERSPECTIVE

This section is about the PESTLE Analysis. As you can see (**Figure.1**), there is a visual representation of the PESTLE Analysis. P.E.S.T.L.E is an acronym for: **P**olitical, **E**conomic, **S**ocial, **T**echnological, **L**egal, and **E**nvironmental.

The PESTLE Analysis, Perspective

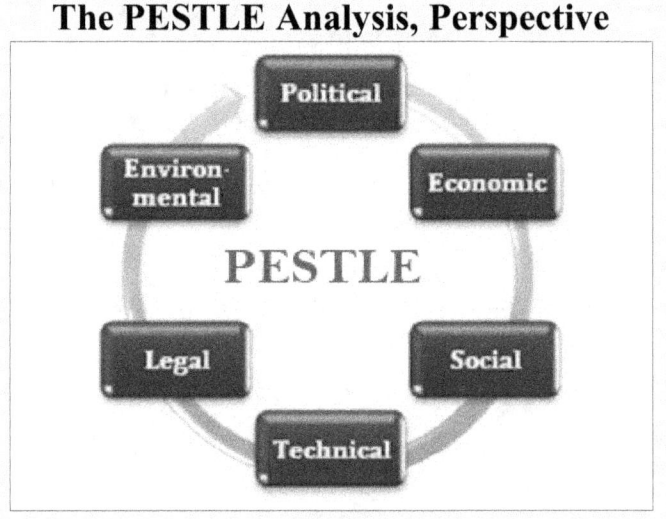

Figure.1: The PESTLE Analysis, Perspective

So in brief, the PESTLE Analysis is an analysis that enables you to carry out a study on an entity from six different perspectives: political, economic, social, technological, legal, and environmental.

We are going to look at its perspectives in some detail as we go along. The objective of the PESTLE Analysis may vary according to the focus of the analysis itself. In other words, it may put more emphasis on the 'economic', or on the 'political', or any of the other six aspects. If the focus is on 'environmental' for example, we use the analysis to identify how external key trends impact on a department, on a company, or, even, on a nation.

Different models, different variations of the PESTLE are used in the analysis: PESTLE, PESTEL, PEST, STEPLE, etc., may be encountered. They are just different ways of referring to this model by different analysts. On the other hand, they all share a common purpose of analyzing the key trends that impact the organization's outside system.

In System's Analysis terms, what is within *the system* - for example the 'company system' - extends to people in the company, the products of the company, its marketing... Whereas the outside of the system (i.e., the external environment of the system) would comprise entities, such as the economy, the weather, etc.

So the models that we mentioned above all have a common purpose of looking at the key trends of the *external environment*: in systems terms, the environment, which impacts the company but, over which the company has no influence. The PESTLE Analysis seeks to focus on those key trends that can impact a department, an enterprise as a whole, or even a global nation if we are carrying out a study internationally.

(Figure.1) provides a visual representation of the PESTLE model: the mind being better at capturing the image than the 'equivalent' text.

With reference to the PESTLE Analysis, the key trends do vary considerably according to the analysis method. So depending on what we are focusing on, the key trends may include: inflation, interest rates, new regulations, air pollution, and the rise of the smartphone. These elements are all in the external environment of the organization and, in the spirit of the PESTLE, we look at how these elements (in the external environment) impact on a department, on the organization as a whole, or on the wider nation.

You may identify key trends and include them in appropriate areas; you could identify different key trends and then group them in some way. This would help with the analysis and would make the analysis a lot smoother if there were such groups that have an impact on the model itself. Thus you would start looking at the impact that the group of elements has on the department or on the enterprise, the impact being positive or negative.

For example, in terms of costs: we would group everything that is related to the cost and then see how this impacts - negatively or positively - on whatever we are studying: a department, or a company, or whatever. Some may have impacts, directly or indirectly, on the company.

In summary, the focus needs to be on the key trends and on quantifying the impact. Therefore, once we have identified the key trends, then we attempt to quantify them and see how they impact the organization under study.

PESTLE Analysis is often used in conjunction with other Analytical Methods which, in fact, complement the analysis of the business environment, for example, the CAGE Analysis. CAGE is an acronym for **C**ulture, **A**dministrative, **G**eographical, and **E**nvironmental. The PESTLE works nicely with the CAGE Analysis and with Porter's Five Forces too. Also, these models are commonly used in pairs; for example,

PESTLE Analysis is often used in pairs with the SWOT Analysis.

What is the SWOT analysis? It is a four-perspective model that focuses on these aspects: **S**trengths, **W**eaknesses, **O**pportunities, and **T**hreats. Note that its elements 'Opportunities' and 'Threats' are external factors of the SWOT Model; they are concerned with the external environment. Therefore, when we are carrying out a PESTLE Analysis, we could consider bringing in the elements 'Opportunities' and 'Threats' of the SWOT model to empower the PESTLE analysis of the entity under study because they too focus on the organization's environment.

PESTLE factors can be classified as Opportunities and Threats; therefore, they would become an integral part of the SWOT analysis. That's why often the best analysis and the SWOT analysis are used as a pair.

The six elements of the PESTLE do not always carry the same weight: we should not think that the key elements (P, E, S, T, L, E) have all got the same weight in the PESTLE Analysis.

The model is very flexible. Moreover, the model is used depending on the situation under study, and so we put more emphasis on the items that we think are more relevant to our analysis. The key element 'social', for example, would relate more closely to the consumer aspect of the analysis. Whereas the key element 'political' is more appropriate in a political study, situation, for example, government, defence, aerospace, and so on.

2. THE PESTLE ANALYSIS - POLITICAL

We have covered a perspective of the PESTLE Analysis, as a strategic tool. Now, we are going to focus its first element, the *'political'* aspect.

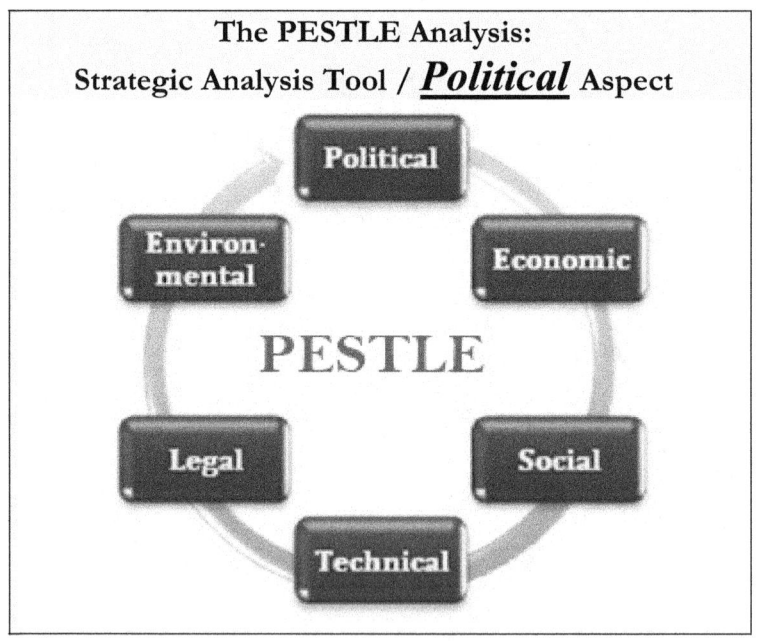

Figure.2: The PESTLE Analysis, the 'Political' aspect

The PESTLE Analysis is a tool, which is often used to scan the external macro environment of the organization under study. It is an important tool that drives the analysis to be focused on the organization from different perspectives, the six different perspectives that make it an important tool.

These perspectives, as we have seen in the visual representation of the PESTLE Analysis (**Figure.1**), do cover these elements: political, economic, social, cultural, technological, legal and environmental. These perspectives help in evaluating the position, the potential and the direction of the business. Therefore, we use this analysis to study the macro environment of the enterprise in order to help evaluate the position, the potential and the direction of the business in question and thus develop a clear picture of the market growth or decline of this business under study.

The political aspects cover how the politics of the country in which the business is based, how they either hinder or help the market. They are concerned for example with the trade deals nationally or internationally and any trade restrictions in place. Government tax policies and possible political stability, stability in the country may come under this category. Therefore, any tax policies or possible political stability or instability of the country may then come under this category of politics within the PESTLE Analysis. Therefore, depending on the nature of the business, the political aspects may be most significant. For example, in cases, such as defence, or aerospace; these usually are integrated within the heritage of the country in question.

3. THE PESTLE ANALYSIS – ECONOMIC

We are going to go through the six perspectives of the PESTLE Analysis; the next one after the 'political' is the *'economic'* perspective (**Figure.3**). This is going to be very short. In fact, most of them will be short, but concise and precise.

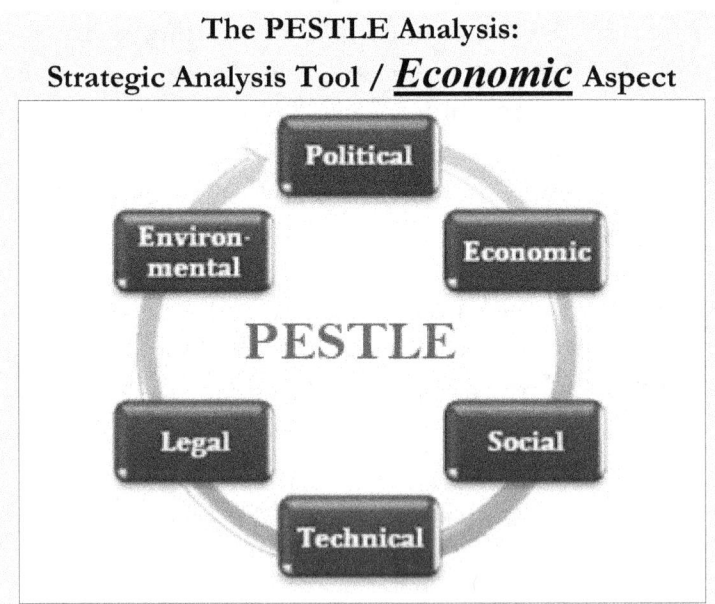

Figure.3: The PESTLE Analysis, the 'Economic' aspect

'Economic' aspects, what are they? They relate to the economic health of the organization, including its purchasing power, it's capital. In addition, they reflect on the economic aspects, such as the economic growth, the exchange, and interest rate, the inflation, etc., therefore; it's obvious, in some way, what the economic aspects are. On the other hand, we need to underline it and put it into focus so that later on when it comes to the implementation of it, we will know what we are dealing with.

4. THE PESTLE ANALYSIS – SOCIAL

Following the PESTLE Analysis, as a strategic analysis tool, we are going to go through the perspectives one by one. After the 'political' and the 'economic' already covered, we are going to tackle the *'social'* perspective of this analysis (**Figure.4**).

Figure.4: The PESTLE Analysis, the 'social' aspect

As the name suggests, the *'social'* aspects relate to the society in which the business operates. That includes consumer needs, the market size for the organization's goods and services, market trends.

The 'social' aspects also cover the population growth of society, its demographics, gender age, etc., and its health matters. Its social aspects vary in significance according to the business market. For example, they are more important if they relate to consumer business or B2B business near the consumer end of the supply chain.

Therefore, the social aspects vary in significance according to the business market. That's the key thing. In addition, that's what we have got to bear in mind.

5. THE PESTLE ANALYSIS - TECHNICAL/TECHNOLOGICAL

Let's move on to the next element of the PESTLE Analysis, its *'technological'* perspective (**Figure.5**).

The PESTLE Analysis:
Strategic Analysis Tool / **Technological** aspect

Figure.5: The PESTLE Analysis, the 'technological' aspect

As previously, short in its description, the ***impact of the technological aspects*** is on the business investment, incentives, innovation, and automation.

They concern its development and its barrier to entry. This applies to the business itself as it does to its competitors.

The technological aspects also cover the make or buy decisions and, moreover, the business technological change, a big change indeed.

6. THE PESTLE ANALYSIS – LEGAL

Let's move on down the series of the perspectives of the PESTLE Analysis; the next element being the *'legal'* perspective (**Figure.6**).

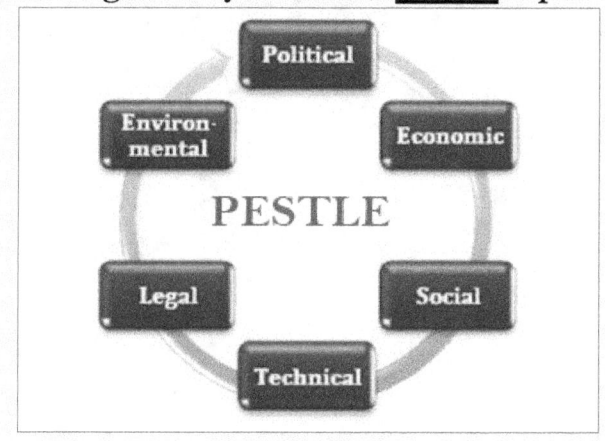

Figure.6: The PESTLE Analysis, the 'legal' aspect

What does the 'legal' perspective consist of?

The *'legal'* aspects of the PESTLE Analysis are concerned by the laws of the land in which the business operates.

They cover government regulations, including tax policies, employment laws environmental regulations, trade laws, and trade restrictions and so on.

7. THE PESTLE ANALYSIS – ENVIRONMENTAL

We have done a full circle and we are now at the last perspective of the PESTLE Analysis, the *'environmental'* perspective (**Figure.7**).

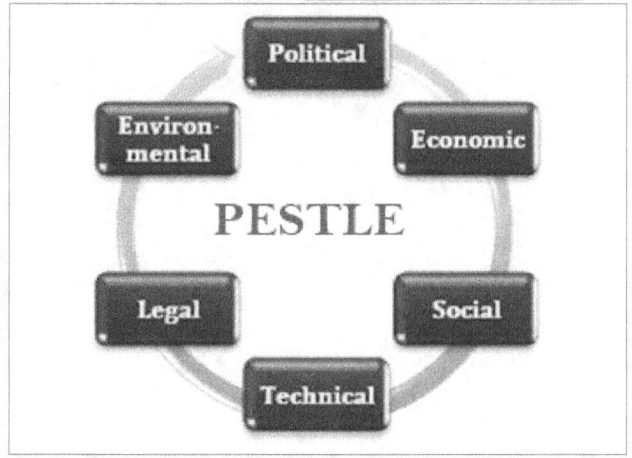

Figure.7: The PESTLE Analysis, the 'environmental' aspect

What do we know about environmental aspects?

The *'environmental'* aspects impact the environment in which the organization operates.

Often, they include critical considerations, depending on the nature of the business: polluting elements, hazardous products, dangerous activities. Therefore, environmental regulations may come under this banner too.

8. PESTLE-ANALYSIS, IMPLEMENTATION ISSUES & OPPORTUNITIES

This part covers the implementation issues and opportunities associated with the PESTLE Analysis, a more pragmatic representation. Moreover, it gives us the opportunity to revisit the model's dimensions, and the model perspectives (**Figure.8**).

Figure.8: The PESTLE Analysis, Implementation issues

The implementation issues cover an interesting part whereby we're going to consider a range of issues that may emerge as we go through the analysis and navigate the

P.E.S.T.L.E perspectives from the P (Political) to the E (Environment).

PESTLE is a framework to attempt to analyze key external factors, factors which do have an impact on most organizations. It is a framework that attempts to focus on the level of competition within the industry of the organization under study. Thus, when we carry out a PESTLE Analysis, we will focus on the level of competition in the industry in which our organization understudy is taking place.

The PESTEL model is often perceived as the ideal tool for such a strategic analysis, driven by these (six) different outside factors that impact on the business: from the political ... to the environmental. All the six perspectives that we have covered.

The PESTLE Analysis could be useful when checking the viability of starting a project. Hence, if we are a start-up company, it could help us to check the viability of our starting project. For example, it could be most helpful in the valuable practice of continuous assessment of issues and risks. Therefore, it could help us to look continuously at the *opportunities* and the *risks (threats)* of a project. Because of these latter two elements, the PESTLE could be a valuable tool, a valuable framework to apply together with, or instead of, the SWOT analysis. This confirms that the PESTLE Analysis goes in pairs with the SWOT, as indicated earlier on.

The PESTLE framework is shown here (**Figure.8**), and it is illustrated through practical examples as will be outlined below.

Therefore, under the *implementation issues title,* the term PESTLE stands for six dimensions, each of which could help bring to light appropriate forces impacting on the business, at different degrees. Therefore, every time we tackle the analysis through one perspective, this would bring to light one side of the enterprise under study. In addition, the model requires the analyst to carry out the analysis (of the entity understudy) - under all its six perspectives - to determine risks, raise issues and identify opportunities; three important points to bear in mind.

Naturally, such exercise would result in some considerable data being brought to the surface for assessment, for analysis.

Why should we consider using the PESTLE Analysis? we do so because the model focuses on the external factors and their impact on the organization. In addition, as pointed out earlier because it is a strategic planning tool that focuses on these outside factors and on how they influence the business understudy. In brief, the PESTLE is used to provide insights into these factors and measures that impact. As such, it concentrates essentially on the macro-environment of the organization and enables the analyst to develop insights into the organization under study.

Let us now revisit the model, build on the introduction of its six perspectives (carried out above), and develop these stages further, starting with the 'political' dimension.

The *'political'* dimension impacts the organization, but not the other way around. It is often concerned with appropriate legislation and government laws (c.f. above); laws that relate to health and safety, trade, consumer regulations, etc., Government and legislators set and specify such laws. They refer to how a government may seek to impact on the country's economy or industry. The government is always attempting to do that because it is their responsibility to manage the country's economy, the country's industry - relating to the entity and the project under study.

Let's give an example for this perspective, an example of issues and opportunities associated with this dimension:

For example, building a long-span bridge. The local government would oversee the project, as a partner, together with local builders and may require that sixty percent (60%) of the suppliers are sourced locally, to drive the local economy. That's a **political** dimension.

Many ***opportunities*** appear to be associated with this dimension. For instance, if the subject is a big project, the government may want to get involved and try and steer the project so that it is most beneficial to the country as a whole. This harnesses various issues, such as localized 'product bill of materials' as well as opportunities 'import taxes savings' etc.

The '*economic;* dimension also covers factors such as interest rates and rate of inflation, factors of unemployment and employment recession, etc., so that's what the economic dimension attempts to cover.

Organizations are continually attempting to influence these external factors directly or indirectly, but they don't always succeed. Often with a negligible rate of success diluting recession effect, countering employment and unemployment fluctuations rates, consumer buying capacity.

In the concept of *systems*, as indicated previously, everything that is inside the system is under the control of the owner of the system. Subsequently, what is outside the system that is in the macro environment of the organization is not under the control of the system and it can influence the system, but the system cannot influence it?

Moreover, the *'economic' dimension* focuses on elements that impact directly on the local and international economy particularly through long term projects. So the *'economic'* direction is concerned especially with long term projects that come directly under the economy direction. The latter is usually controlled by the government.

Issues and Opportunities associated with the 'economic' dimension could include, for example, a rise in inflation or fluctuating exchange rates between the US dollar and the euro, or between the euro and other currencies. This rise of inflation or fluctuating exchange rate (U.S. dollar/Euros etc.) could impact a supply chain project such that it demands more money to complete the project or conversely benefits from this change creating an opportunity in money-saving in materials.

Let's look at the *social/sociological* dimension now.

This dimension often impinges on others, such as the *economic* one above where consumer buying power and social factors are interrelated. Therefore, the *sociological* dimension impacts, particularly on the *economic* dimension. Dimension and perspectives are used interchangeably here throughout the book.

Consumer buying products has a social dimension: why people buy what they buy. This is researched by companies for effective marketing: tuning their product to the market, to the right market, to the right people. And effective marketing will not be effective without insights into the social elements, such as culture, ethnicity, health, education, social background, etc.

It's not an easy task for organizations to change social factors; organizations often try to adapt to the social factors, but not change them. Although they may attempt to do so. Organizations turn instead towards observing and studying such social factors. Therefore, as was indicated earlier on, for their marketing to be effective they need to adapt their products to the market, and so that they can sell more easily to the consumer, the social unit.

Observe, study, adapt and sell are all activities aimed at understanding the consumer needs and solving his problems. So to solve the consumer problem we need to observe this society (this society unit), study it, adapt our products to it and sell it into it. '*Social*' dimension concerns the *social* and *cultural* scenarios associated with the project in hand.

An example of issues and opportunities associated with this dimension:

A Chinese team set to build a long-span bridge in the UK. Of course, the managers from China may encounter a culture of shock at first, or experience issues related to the local union in the face of the British culture.

The ***'Technological'*** perspective: it relates to technical issues and information technology, which raise complications, require solutions or call for improvement on innovation in any environment, such as manufacturing, cyber-security, telecommunications: so different backgrounds, different sectors.

Organizations seek competitive advantage, that's the driving force behind every organization. If it hasn't got a competitive advantage then it cannot go very far. Technology, at its best, could help the organization through: better products and services, enhanced Customer Relations Management (CRM), agile human resource management, improvement, and innovation. Therefore, technology can help the organization to develop a competitive advantage in these sectors and many others.

The *'technology'* dimension is essentially concerned with the technology, with the innovation factors that may impact on the success of the project under study. It may impact it negatively or positively.

Example of a new untested technology/device *that may offer an opportunity of empowering the project in hand and/or reducing its associated costs extensively.*

The **'*legal*'** perspective: whenever we talk about legal, that's the law. What laws and legislation will impact on the type of organization understudy? That's the question we should raise when we are carrying out the PESTLE Analysis under this *legal* perspective. The *'political'* perspective covered above has already addressed an important part of the '*legal*' one too. '*Political*' and '*legal*' are intertwined, and they impinge on one another.

The '*political*' is also concerned with appropriate legislation and government laws: government and legislators set and specify such laws. These laws impact on the organization, but not the other way around. Remember that: because they are in the macro-environment and that, therefore, the organization that is within the system is impacted by the laws of the government. The *legal* dimension relating to the laws that can influence the project considered either as issues or opportunities. Note that: 'Issues or Opportunity', this makes us think of 'Opportunities and Threats of the SWOT model.

Example of an issue *whereby you want to extend your business to a country where the law of that country requires you to go on a partnership, based on a 50 percent ownership by a local investor. Some countries will, if you want to set up a business in that country, make you go in a partnership with a local company, which will then own fifty percent (50%) of the business. This may delay the business launch and later diminish your responsibility and control in the company. Therefore, 50 - 50 ownership, means you set up the business in that country, but you don't have the full control over that business because your partner has got fifty percent (50%) of the control and you have got fifty percent (50%) of it.*

The '*environmental*', which is going to be the last dimension/perspective of the PESTLE Analysis. What environmental ecological and green factors will impact on the type of the organization under study, locally and beyond? So we ask ourselves the question: how will this put an impact on the type of the organization under study locally and beyond.

Different organizations are more or less concerned or impacted by this *environmental* perspective. We may find that the giant oil company is directly impacted by such an *environmental* perspective because it could cause chaos in the waters of the Atlantic, for example.

Oil companies, Mining organizations, Agricultural entities, Chemical plants, each of these types of organizations are heavily impacted by this *environmental* perspective. By comparison, Local Schools may be concerned by this perspective, but they are not necessarily impacted by it.

The *environment* dimension extends to factors, such as weather, climate, and global changes, geography or whatever environment characteristics impinging on the project considered.

Example: Agricultural projects. *What is agriculture without an environmental perspective? So the agricultural entities are heavily impacted by this dimension. Chemical manufacturing plants and similar entities would fall into this category where the average weather and temperature may lead to risks or opportunities factors, but not to the extent of an agricultural entity.*

9. APPLYING PESTLE ANALYSIS-1

This section addresses the implementation of the PESTLE Analysis.

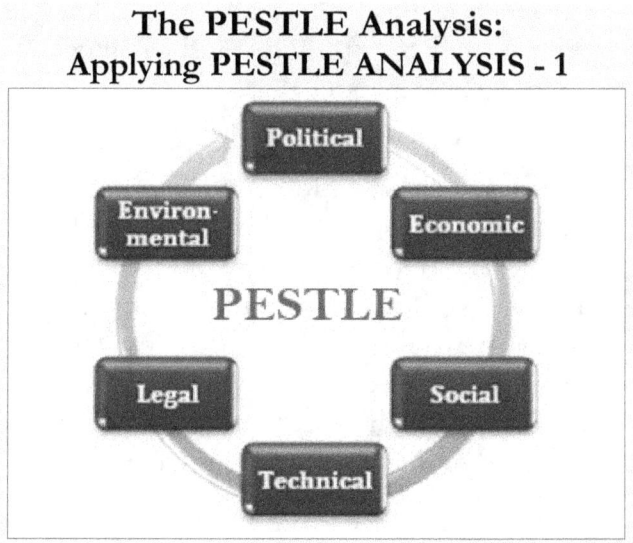

Figure.9: Applying the PESTLE Analysis1

There will be two parts that complement one another: Applying PESTLE Analysis-1 and Applying PESTLE Analysis-2. These have been separated on purpose to make them individually more manageable.

Back to the PESTLE Analysis with its six perspectives (**Figure.9**). Here the latter will be covered from an implementation perspective: the application of the model.

Applying PESTLE Analysis involves us in looking at the data. Data is the basis for the analysis. The analyst gathers the data required to launch the analysis process. This may be achieved through data capture, for example: brainstorming and competitor analysis.

The competitor analysis, for example, would address the competitor's data that focus on specific target issues that are relevant to our business. For the organization, some issues may need to be understood and acted upon or improved, for example, selling points, perceived strengths, and weaknesses. Note that these last two elements ('Strengths and Weaknesses') constitute the force of the SWOT model.

Now, applying the PESTLE Analysis proper involves the analyst in viewing the organization under study from different perspectives, the six perspectives. These are inherent in the acronyms P.E.S.T.L.E (Political, Economic, Social, Technological, Legal, and Environmental), which suggests breaking the analysis down into related (six) categories. Therefore, by proceeding in this way, applying the PESTLE Analysis under its different facets helps to derive the data into chunks, into categories that are manageable, that makes sense.

Let's see how this translates into each of the six perspectives.

- Implementation related to the *'political'* perspective: how would the analyst, using the PESTLE Analysis, view the organization under the *political* umbrella? The analyst would focus here on what opportunities and pressures political bodies bring about, and to what degree public regulations do impact on the business understudy.

In assessing this first perspective '*political*' we may need to consider the different laws that bear on the business under study: those laws already complied with, and those that you have yet to bring on board.

Therefore, we view the organization under the umbrella of *politics* and make our assessment. We look into the laws that have actually been implemented and those that are yet to be brought on board.

What would be the impact of the latter (to-be), if they were or were not complied with? In answer to this question, we look at their impact, in case they are present or in the case they are not. An assessment from this perspective is the first part of the PESTLE Analysis. Obviously, we have got to be a lawful organization, therefore, the PESTLE Analysis addresses this *political* aspect in the first instance.

- Implementation related to the '*economical*' perspective: this perspective asks, at this stage, what structures, trends, and economic policies do affect the organization? And, to what degree?

The PESTLE approach proposes to consider the *economic* factors. Therefore, when we are using the PESTLE Analysis, we are focusing on the *economic* factors, which range from taxes, rates inflation, market trends and other influences of the economy. We have covered some of those before, but we are now pulling all this information together and structuring in the context of 'implementation'.

Pertinent questions can be raised. These are raised for more insights, about things like inflation. How is inflation affecting the organization? How is the recession affecting the organization? How are the taxes affecting the organization? What tax band should the organization be in? Are the inflation rates so high as to affect the product's production and distribution? Or will a coming recession impact sales or growth?

Note that inflation, taxes, recession are entities outside the (organization) system.

- Implementation related to the *'sociological'* perspective (i.e., social or sociological). Under this umbrella of *'sociological'*, we consider the enterprise understudy from '*culture*' and '*society*' point of view. We will be looking at the '*culture*' and '*society*' attributes and their effect on the organization's product and processes.

Therefore, we think here essentially about consumers and draw on target market research results, seeking to develop insights into the buying trends. Thus, we need to look at the consumers:

- What they buy and why they buy it
- From the flow of goods and services within the organization's target market.

A particular focus on the *competitors* and the *suppliers* of competitive products is pertinent to the analysis, from this *sociological* perspective. We should ask questions such as: ----- should the organization under study take advantage of any of the competitor's failures? Therefore, what they are doing well is something to worry about. But, we also need to look at their weaknesses and exploit them so that they become our Strengths and give us a *competitive advantage*. In other words, we avoid their pitfalls; and seek to be seen under a better, more favourable light by the customer: more favourable equates to having a competitive advantage.

- Implementation related to the *'technological'* perspective: the *technological* aspects of the organization, together with the associated barriers incentives and innovation, do have a strong impact on the organization's operation and performance. Therefore, they need a particular attention, bearing in mind that *technology* is extremely important in the marketing and all the operations of the organization.

The technological perspective is thus addressed with a greater attention. It follows on from the *social* one (above); they go hand-in-hand. The *technology* often gets inspiration from the *sociological* aspects. Here, we need to raise some pertinent questions, which will lead to comprehending the *technology* dimension of the organization under study. To do so, it is most appropriate to use the 5 Ws (What? When? Why? Where? Who? How?). Hence, when we are dealing with our *technological* aspects of the analysis, the 5Ws may prove to be very handy. they may not in other circumstances. Let's ask our pertinent questions indicated above:

- For example, what *technology* does the organization use, at both an operational and strategic level?

Therefore, we look at the technology from the tactical and from the strategic point of view, and we raise questions such as:

- **What** *technology is being used from both the above angles?*
- **Why** *is this very technology used in the organization in comparison to the competition?*

In short, we look at what the competition is using in terms of technology and we ask why they are using it and you are not, or why you are both using it. By asking such questions, we are going to develop some good insights into the organization under study.

- **Where** *is the technology most concentrated?*

  Are we using our technology mostly in this field and not in the other? Should it be the other way around? Should you develop what you are using in this field into the other field, which is lacking in performance?

- **When** *is it the technology maintained and updated?*

[It's well and good having technology in the application, but if it is not maintained and not updated, it would be more a hinder rather than a help].

- ***How*** does it impact the business at this level?

    [So, we look at the technology at different levels of the organization and see how it impacts on each of those levels].

- ***How*** will existing technology reduce costs, but increase productivity?

    [So we are looking at how best technology is used within the organization, with the purpose of increasing productivity and reducing the cost to increase profit margins, and that's what business should focus on].

We have got two dimensions that are left with regard to the complete model, the PESTLE Analysis model, the ***legal*** and the ***environmental***.

The ***legal***: here we ask some questions such as:

- ***What*** laws and legislation will impact on our kind of organization.
    [Focus on appropriate legislation and government laws].

With regard to the ***environmental***:

Depending on the nature of the business understudy, we analyze here what environmental and ecological assets do impact strongly on our business, locally and far afield.

We may not be so concerned with the environmental aspect during our analysis but, by raising the question, we may discover some important facts that we probably have neglected before now.

In general, PESTLE may be used globally as a strategic tool, as indicated previously. Why? For the purpose of understanding the business position, potential, and direction, for operations market growth or decline. Therefore, globally that's what the PESTLE Analysis seeks to do.

In particular, we focus our attention on the external analysis. In addition, if one tool could be effective at looking at the external analysis, the PESTLE Analysis would be such a tool.

While carrying out the market's study or strategic assessment, it would help to build an overview of wide-ranging macro-environmental attributes; we said all along that's where the power of the PESTLE Analysis is. It is in the macro-environmental attributes of the organization. And the organization using the PESTLE Analysis should carefully consider these macro-environmental attributes. This exercise could effectively benefit our organization from available opportunities and help it avoid potential threats.

At this stage, we may want to do a SWOT analysis (SWOT: Strengths, Weaknesses, Opportunities, and Threats). Therefore, we may want, at this particular point of the PESTLE Analysis stage. Such PESTLE based study - that's with the external analysis in focus - provides important results that the organization should take into consideration, measure and use towards the positive impact that this may have on the organization.

10. APPLYING PESTLE ANALYSIS-2

This section is about the PESTLE Analysis part two (**Figure.10**). It is going to be done on what we have already covered so far.

**The PESTLE Analysis:
Applying PESTLE ANALYSIS - 2**

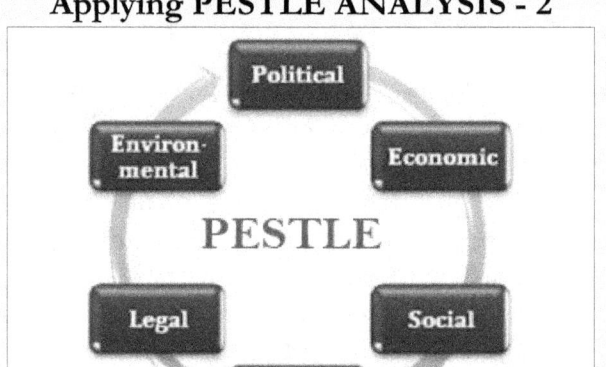

Figure.10: Applying the PESTLE Analysis2

The PESTLE Analysis may follow the procedure depicted by (**Figure.11**), through these shown stages.

Applying PESTLE Analysis -2

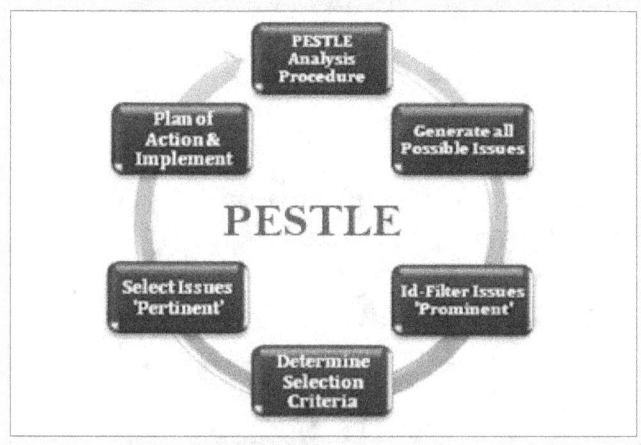

Figure.11: Applying the PESTLE Analysis2, Stages

Before you (**Figure.11**) is the procedure that is worthwhile following to carry out the PESTLE Analysis and structure its deployment. This approach will you gain time and steer you in the right direction.

As shown (**Figure.11**),

- We start off by element "Zero" of the diagram, the *'PESTLE Analysis procedure'*.
- Thereafter, we launch with (stage.1), *'generate possible issues'*.
- These issues are *filtered* at (stage.2), to *'create prominent issues'*.
- The procedure leads on, then, to *'determine a selection criteria'* (stage.3),
- Then we carry out the *'selection pertinent issues'* (stage.4), and,
- End up by *'create a Plan of Action, and Implement'*, [i.e., a Gant Chart] (stage.5).

Applying PESTLE Analysis -2:
[The PESTLE Analysis, Procedure]

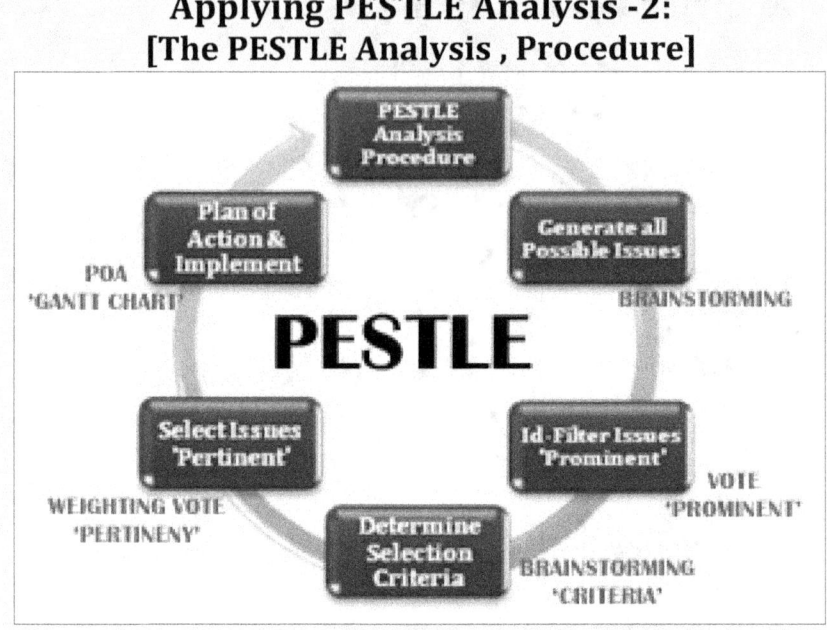

Figure.12: Applying the PESTLE Analysis2, Procedure

This is the chain of events; how can this be realized?

- To generate all *the possible issues*, we could use some data capture form, such as a *brainstorming*, for example. Through a brainstorming session, we generate all the *possible issues*, and then,
- We move on to launch a vote, with a view of deriving the *prominent issues* (from the above *possible issues*).
- We then proceed to the next stage to determine a *criteria selection*. Another *brainstorming* exercise can be used for this purpose.
- A *weighting vote* can now be applied to the *prominent issues* (derived above)
- Using the *selected criteria* determined above
- To bring out *'pertinent issues'*.

As a matter of interest, a *weighting vote* is a vote whereby we do assign different weights (coefficients) to different elements, according to their importance, cost, efficiency, etc. In our case, certain criteria end up weighing more than certain others, as a result of the *weighting vote*.

- Finally, a *Plan of Action*, a Gantt Chart, for example, may now be set up to proceed to the implementation of these derived work results.

We have thus developed a complete procedure for applying the PESTLE Analysis, a procedure not intended to be rigid, but to be used as a flexible and effective guide to carry out the analysis process.

Let's develop the different activities used throughout the procedure stages (introduced above).

The *brainstorming* activity (**Figure.13**):

The first entity that we are going to look at is *generating all the possible issues*. How? By using a data capture, such as the *brainstorming*.

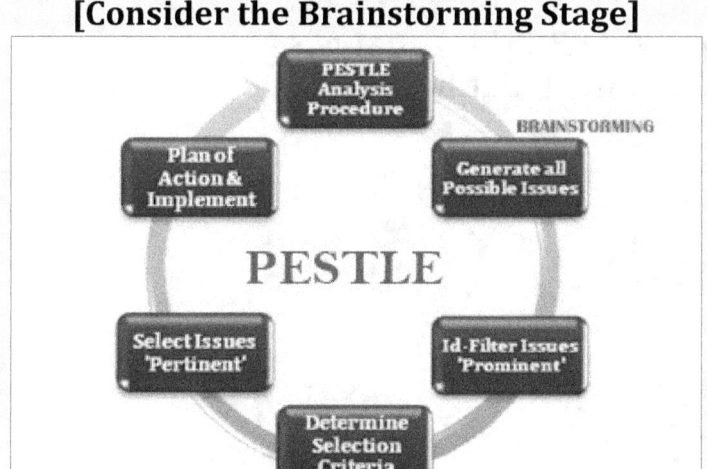

**Applying PESTLE Analysis -2:
[Consider the Brainstorming Stage]**

Figure.13: PESTLE Analysis2, Procedure - Brainstorming

In effect, the procedure starts off with a *brainstorming* exercise. This requires that the team members concerned, gather together to generate maximum ideas. These ideas correspond to all the *possible issues* and opportunities; the different points raised by the team members. So this is step one of the procedure.

Remember this is only a guide and not something you have to adhere to rigidly during the PESTLE Analysis process.

Let's move on to the next stage: *brainstorming identification/filtering*

In the procedure, this is as shown (**Figure.14**). **W**hat is it about? It is a stage whereby we will *filter the possible issues* that we have identified; to filter out those factors most relevant, to remove duplications of ideas, and to combine those that have the same meaning, the same purpose.

At this stage, the resulting list of ideas is put to the *vote* to determine the most *prominent issues*, to create a *prominent list*.

Applying PESTLE Analysis -2:
[Filtering / Identification Stage]

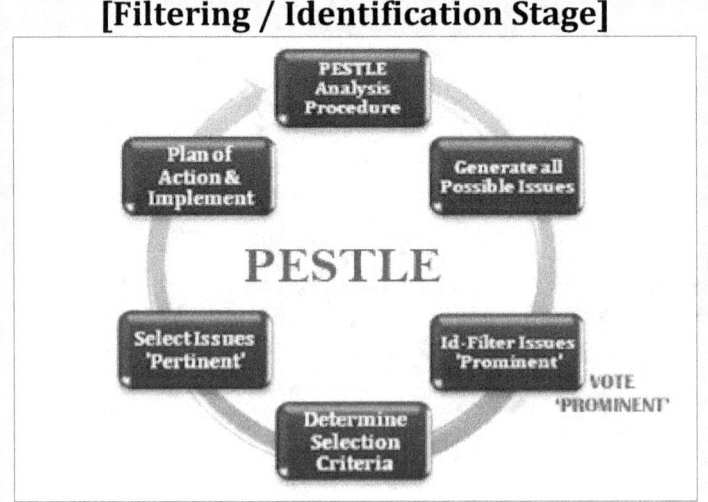

Figure.14: PESTLE Analysis2, Procedure - Vote Brainstorming

The next stage is concerned with: *importance and impact rating* as depicted by (Figure.15).

Applying PESTLE Analysis -2:
[Importance / Impact Rating Stage]

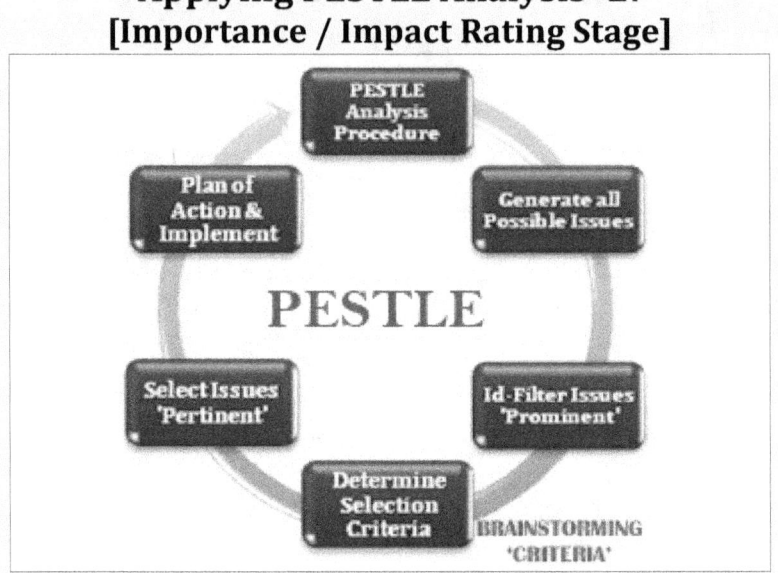

Figure.15: PESTLE Analysis2, 'Impact Rating'

The *Prominent List* above is put through a kind of credibility test whereby each idea is assessed for its *impact/importance*; each idea is assessed according to its impact and importance.

For this, we carry out a *brainstorming* to decide which *criteria* are most relevant and establish a resulting *criteria-list* (a set of coefficients). Next, we will apply this latter *criteria-list (of coefficients)*, to analyze and to assess the *impact and the importance* of each one of the ideas in the *prominent list*.

Armed with the *prominent list* and the *set of criteria (above)*, we will apply the latter to the former, the *set of criteria* to the *prominent list of ideas*, to generate a *pertinent list (of ideas)*.

We have moved through this PESTLE Analysis procedure, from the *weighted vote* to the *prominent list*, to the most *pertinent issues*; and now we carry out a *weighted vote* - (**Figure.16**).

Applying PESTLE Analysis -2:
[Likelihood / Probability Assessment]

Figure.16: PESTLE Analysis2, 'Weighted Vote'

What is a '*weighted vote*'? it is no different from an ordinary vote, apart from the fact that its elements, being voted on, are given different coefficients (criteria) according to their impact/importance. In effect, not all resulting votes (from the *weighting vote*) are of equal importance. We vote for an item that may have a weight more relevant than another to determine the most *prominent list*.

So we want to move from the *prominent list* to the most *pertinent list (of issues / ideas)*, and that process is achieved through the *weighted vote*.

We move on, therefore, from this stage, armed with the *pertinent list* to our **Plan of Action** for implementation and execution of the results thus achieved (**Figure.17**).

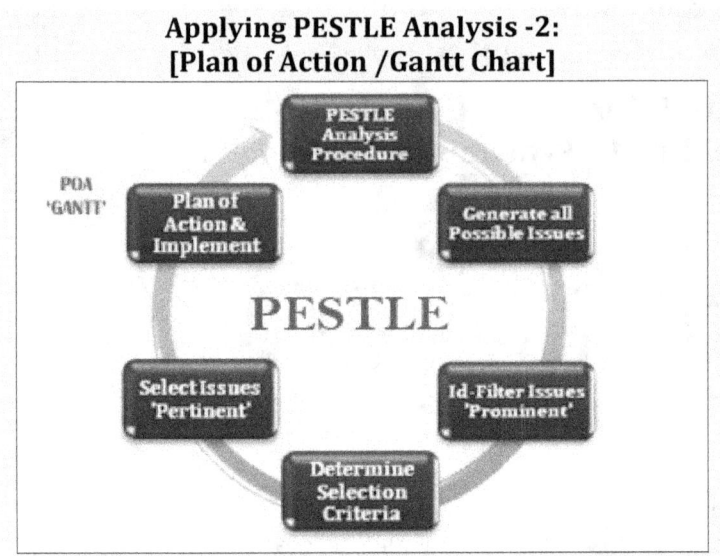

Figure.17: PESTLE Analysis2, 'Plan of Action'

Notes:

This *Plan of Action* **(PoA)** could be in the form of a **Gantt Chart**. It is subsequently implemented and executed by the team, for the purpose of avoiding issues or exploiting opportunities.

1) - This PESTLE Analysis procedure is cyclic. That means, if we are not happy with any of the results at any stage, we will move on and do one around again through the loop.

2) - This is not the PESTLE Analysis proper, but a method that is used by the PESTLE Analysis.

In summary of the PESTLE Analysis procedure (Figure.18):

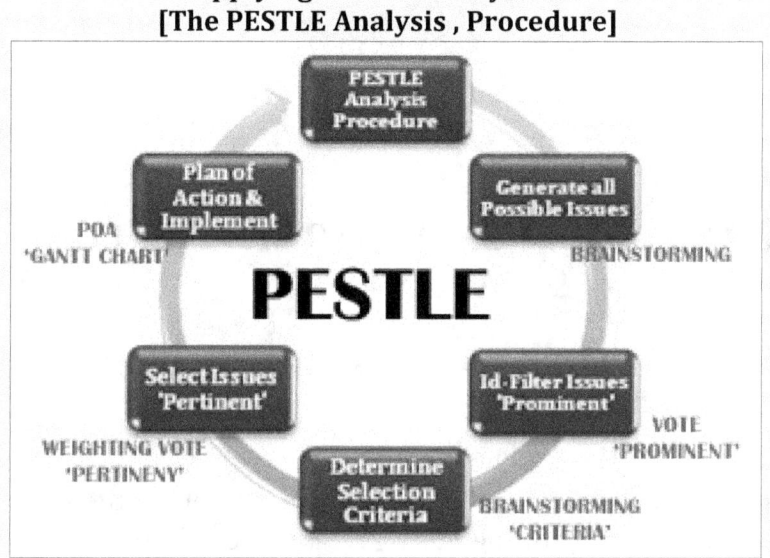

Figure.18: PESTLE Analysis2, 'Procedure'

It generates *possible ideas and issues* through a *brainstorming* exercise.

Then it takes the result and applies a *vote* to determine a *prominent list*.

Then, it moves on to *identify a set of criteria* using again the *brainstorming* and that determines a *pertinent list*, through a *weighting vote*.

The resulting *pertinent list* will then be implemented through a *Plan of Action* (a Gantt chart).

11. PRACTICE: PESTLE-ARCHITECTURE & CASE STUDY

Applying Business Analysis tools is our focus; it is a central theme of this book.

Let us now apply the six perspectives of the P.E.S.T.L.E Model to a real situation case study. We seek to apply them, one perspective at a time, through using a case study about Algeria.

The PESTLE Analysis: 'Case Study'
Country Background, Algeria

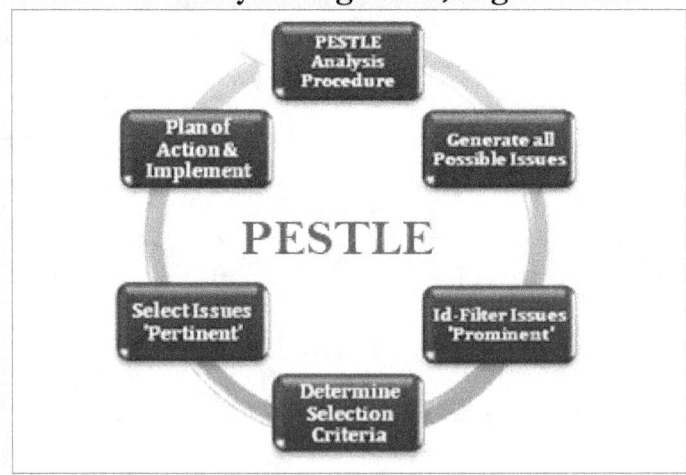

Figure.19: PESTLE Analysis2, 'Case Study-1: Algeria'

Algeria is a country in North Africa and we are applying the PESTLE Analysis to the case study, from what we know about Algeria.

We will be looking at it from the six different perspectives: *'political'*, *'economic'*, *'social'*, *'technological'*, *'legal'* and *'environmental'*. Each of these will be an appropriate **keyword** through the analysis.

You may consult the overall case study in (**Annex-A**), although there is sufficient information provided here through the different figures below to enable you to follow the analysis.

Table.1: PESTLE Analysis, 'Case Study-1: Algeria'

\multicolumn{4}{c}{The PESTLE Analysis: Case Study 'Algeria'}
PESTLE	Background (Specific attributes)	Algeria EC Key Issues	S.W.O.T
P-Political	- A black decade (of terrorism) impacted politics	- e-Government [***]	- Threat
	- Country moved from Socialist to Capitalist	- e-Government [**]	- Opportunity
	- Democracy: at infancy stage	- e-Government [*]	- Opportunity
	- Corruption heavy, and at various levels (see social)	- e-Government [**]	- Weakness/ Threat
E-Economic	As above, with the following specific points:		
	- Country: Developing	- e-Trade[***]	- Opportunity
	- Public companies dominate market vs. Private	- e-Trade[*]	- Weakness
	- CRM culture poor (see Social)	- CRM/ e-Marketing[**]	- Threat
	- Banking system inefficient/ e-banking missing	- e-Trade[**]	- Threat
	- SCM (logistics most inefficient, when existing)	- e-Trade[**]	- Weaknesses
	- Currency: Algerian Dinar, not convertible	- e-banking/ e-banking[*]	- Weakness
	- Inflation: officially declared around 3%, in reality in double figures	- e-Trade[**]	- Threat ....
Keys:	[*]=Weak ; [**]: Moderate; [***]: Strong		
EC Key Issues	e-Government, e-Trade, CRM, e-payment (e-banking), e-Marketing, Human Resources, Social Networks, Culture, ICT, Legislation (legal),		

Algeria's Background:

Algeria is the fourth richest country of Africa, having two hundred sixty-eight thousand nine hundred ($268900) dollars GDP; while the GDP per capita of Algeria is 134. 797 billion dollars (as estimated by the IMF in 2009).

The fossil fuels energy sector is the backbone of Algeria's economy, accounting for roughly 60% of budget revenues, 30% of GDP and over 90% of export earnings.

"Algeria ranks 14th in petroleum reserves, containing over 11 billion barrels of proven oil reserves; with estimates suggesting that the actual amount is even more" (www.africaspotlight.com)

The purpose of the case study:

The analysis was carried out on Algeria e-commerce in particular. So we will not look at Algeria from every angle. We will look at it from the e-commerce point of view only.

Therefore, this PESTLE Analysis was carried out, against the above background of the country, having in mind that we are interested in the key element, e-commerce. You may do another study with a different focus than e-commerce, of course. The objective to underline the validity and reliability of the key findings of the study against the said background, so as to ensure the findings are what they appear to be.

(**Table.1**) is a comprehensive table, which (so far) only addresses the *political* and *economic* aspects (the keywords) of the Analysis, as you can see from (**Colum.1**).

(**Column.2**) shows the *elements* (*specific attributes*) that we have pulled out from the case study itself, point by point, mapping them to our two *keywords* above: *political* and *economic* (of **Column.1**).

In more details, we have identified, against the aspect '*political*', (Column.1) the following specific attributes (see Column.2):

- *a black decade of terrorism that impacted Algeria: its politics and its civilian life,*
- *also, we have underlined that the country has moved from a socialist to a capitalist country;*
- *that the country is at its infancy stage, as far as democracy is concerned.*
- *that corruption is heavy and at various levels.*

In short, these *specific attributes* are the *key elements* that we have identified - from the background of Algeria - against the *political* perspective. Therefore, that's how we carry out our analysis under the umbrella of each of the six perspectives of the PESTLE model.

(**Column.3**) shows the *'key issues'* that were identified from the background study. These (shown in *italics*) are related to the specific attributes' (of **Column.2**). This step is optional and specific to the analysis in hand because the k*ey issues* shown are issues that the author wanted to keep in mind as complementary information. You may want to skip this step altogether or substitute it with your own specific requirements.

What is worth addressing though, is how the SWOT model (**Column.4**) could be introduced to empower the analysis. The SWOT may prove to work effectively and in harmony with the PESTLE Analysis. How does it help bring some insights into the 'specific attributes' identified (**Column.2**)? And, subsequently, how does it help enhance the PESTLE Analysis drive?

Let us focus on the '*political*' perspective of the PESTLE Model (Column.1) and,

It's the first related *'specific attribute'* (**Column.2**, *'black decade of terrorism impacted politics'*:

- This is an 'e-government' *key issue* and it has three (3) stars (**Column.3**), which indicates that this *key issue* is a strong one.

- What does the SWOT tell us about that? The SWOT sees this as a 'Threat' because the SWOT is only interested in Strengths, Weaknesses, Opportunities, and Threats.

Let's look at the next *'specific attribute': country moved from socialist to capitalist* (**Column.2**).

- The *key issue* is 'e-government', with two (2) stars, (**Column.3**) it is thus moderate.

- What does the SWOT say about this? It sees an 'Opportunity' **(Column.4)** in this country move: from socialism to capitalism. Hence the mention of Opportunity (next to it).

Now, consider the *'specific attribute'*: *'democracy at its infancy stage'*

- From the SWOT point of view, yes this is an 'Opportunity' (**Column.4**).

- And, we are still under *e-government,* but with one (1) star rating (**Colum.3**); this *key issue* is a weak one, not that important.

Now, consider the next *'specific attribute'*: *'corruption is heavy in the country and at various levels'*.

- Yes, it is an *e-government* '*key issue*' of two (2) stars rating, thus moderate (**Column.3**).

- What does the SWOT say? It says (**Column.4**) that we have got here a *Weakness*, which may be a *Threat*.

Moving on from the first perspective of the PESTLE model (*political*) to its second perspective, '*economic*' (Column.1).

Therefore, let's look at the Algeria background from an ***economic*** perspective.

- The first *'specific attribute'* identified here, with respect to the '*economic*' perspective is 'country is developing' (**Column.2**).

- It is an *e-trade* '*key issue*' of three (3) stars rating, thus strong (**Column.3**).

- What does the SWOT say about it? It says (**Column.4**) that we have got an *opportunity* here.

Let's move on to the next '*specific attribute*': *Public companies dominate the market, versus private " (this is because the country was a social country).*

- It is an *e-trade* '*key issue*' of one (1) star rating, thus weak (**Column.3**). {Maybe it's not *weak* and you would not agree with this assessment, and that the rating should be three (3) stars, from your point of view. Different views are acceptable}.

- What does the SWOT say about it? It says (**Column.4**) that we have got a Weakness here (because you cannot go very far as the economy of the country, with 'the companies being owned by the government ').

The following '*specific attribute*' to address: '*CRM (Customer Relations Management) culture poor*' (**Column.2**).

CRM: Algeria is a poor culture country; the CRM is not such an important thing in the country and

- The '*key issue*' shown (**Column.3**) is *CRM* and *e-marketing*, with a two (2) stars rating, thus moderate.

- What can the SWOT tell us about it? It says (**Column.4**) that it is a *Threat*. If we carry out an analysis here using the SWOT, we would determine that there is a Threat. Note: you may not agree with this assessment, what matters is you justify your reasoning. This is not exact sciences; it is based on the analyst's own analysis approach, his perception, and judgement.

The next '*specific attribute*' to consider is: '*banking system inefficient/ e-banking missing* (**Column.2**).

- The '*key issue*' shown (**Column.3**) is *e-Trade* with a two (2) stars rating, thus moderate.

- How does the SWOT view this? It views this (**Column.4**) as a *Threat*; particularly because e-Trade without e-payment is a no winner. In addition, what is your view on the matter?

(**Column.2**) shows the next '*specific attribute*' being: *SCM (Supply Chain Management) logistics most inefficient when existing*': that is they are practically non-existent, and when they are, they are most inefficient.

- The '*key issue*' shown (**Column.3**) is *e-Trade* with a two (2) stars rating, thus moderate.

- How does the SWOT view this? It views this (**Column.4**) as a *Threat*; particularly because of e-Trade without efficient SCM id doomed to fail.

Let us look at the following '*specific attribute*': '*Currency: the Algerian it is not convertible*' **Column.3**):

- The '*key issue*' shown (**Column.3**) is e-banking and e-payment with a one (1) star rating: weak.

- How does the SWOT view this? It views this (**Column.4**) as a *Weakness*; it certainly is a Weakness if we consider a situation with no e-banking, no e-payment, and the national currency not convertible.

The next '*specific attribute*' deals with: '*Inflation: officially declared around 3 percent, but in reality in double figures*' **Column.3**):

- The '*key issue*' shown (**Column.3**) is e-Trade with a two (2) stars rating: moderate.

- What can we tell from a SWOT perspective? (**Column.4**) shows this to be a *Threat*; It certainly is a Threat to the economy and beyond (because of such numbers play with official statistics). We have a *moderate* issue, but the T*hreat* is considerable from the SWOT point of view.

We have thus studied (**Table-1**) every '*key issue*' (**Column.3**), related to every '*specific attribute*' (**Column.2**), with regard to both perspectives of the PESTLE model: *Political* and **Economic** (**Column.1**) and used the SWOT model (**Column.4**), for further insights into our analysis.

Let's move on now to the third perspective of the PESTLE model, the *social* perspective (Table.2).

(**Column.2**) considers the *'specific attribute'*: *a black decade of terrorism affected Algeria'*, this we are familiar with, as we have addressed it before, but from a different angle. This time, we will focus on it with the ' *Human Resources'* being the *'key issue'* instead (**Column.3**): Human Resources do come under the PESTLE perspective 'social' (**Column.1**).

- The *'key issue'* is thus (**Column.3**) Human Resources, with three (3) stars rating: strong.

- What about the SWOT insight? (**Column.4**): it shows a *Threat*; It certainly is a *Threat* because most of the intellectuals of Algeria left the country; they migrated because of the terrorism. Therefore, there is a big threat in there today and tomorrow. Note that 'the decade of terrorism' is over and has been over for 10 years now. Although we are looking at Algeria at that time, the brain drain impact is still affecting the country.

Table.2: PESTLE Analysis, 'Case Study-1: Algeria, Part.2'

\multicolumn{4}{c}{The PESTLE Analysis: Case Study 'Algeria'}			
PESTLE	Background (Specific attributes)	*Algeria EC Key Issues*	S.W.O.T
S-Social	- A 'black decade' (of terrorism) affected Algeria	- *Human Resources* [***]	- Threat
	- Corruption heavy, and at various levels	- *Human Resources* [**]	- Threat
	- Culture (Islam) strong, but with minor resistance	- *Human Resources* [*]	- Opportunity
	- Illiteracy very high indeed: up-to 11 Million	- *Social Networks* [***]	- Threat
	- Language: Arabic Dialect (Arabic) predominates/	- *Culture* [**]	- Opportunity
	- Arabic: limited /French: limited	- *Culture* [*]	- Weaknesses /

				Threat
T- Technical	- ICT , good standard: DSL, Fiber optic, Computers		- ICT[**]	- Opportunity/ Weakn./Threat
	- Internet: low penetration		- ICT [*]	- Opportunity
	- Mobile Telephony: widespread		- ICT[*]	- Weakness
	- Computer illiteracy, high		- ICT[**]	- Threat
Keys:	[*]=Weak ; [**]: Moderate; [***]: Strong			
EC Key Issues	e-Government, e-Trade, CRM, e-payment (e-banking), e-Marketing, Human Resources, Social Networks, Culture, ICT, Legislation (legal),			

The next '*specific attribute*' considered is: '*Corruption is heavy, and at various levels*' (**Column.2**):

- The '*key issue*' shown (**Column.3**) is '*Human Resources*' with a two (2) stars rating: moderate.

- What can we tell from a SWOT perspective? (**Column.4**) shows this to be a *Threat*; It is no doubt a *Threat* because heavy Corruption destroys the fabric of society, affects its way of life and its Human Resources. What do you think?

(**Column.2**) identifies the '*specific attribute*' to be: '*Culture (Islam) strong, but there is minor resistance*'.

- The '*key issue*' shown (**Column.3**) is '*Human Resources*' with a one (1) star rating: weak

- How about the SWOT insights into the analysis? (**Column.4**) shows this to be an *Opportunity*. Culture Islam is the religion of the country; being strong with minor resistance makes the key issue of '*human resources*' an *Opportunity* because of the *minor resistance* characteristic, which might be explored, exploited and turned it into something positive.

The next '*specific attribute*' addressed is: '*Illiteracy is very high indeed: up to 11 million*' (**Column.2**):

- The *'key issue'* shown (**Column.3**) is *'Social Networks'* with a three (3) stars rating: strong.

- From a SWOT perspective, (**Column.4**), there is a *Threat*. Indeed *Illiteracy* is a big *Threat* from different angles, in general, and from a social perspective, in particular. A threat, if not today it will be lurking in the background for tomorrow, and it may be for a long time.

<u>Also, remember</u>: we are looking at Algeria, from the angle of 'e-commerce' and at the country as a whole.

(**Column.2**) shows the next *'specific attribute'* being: *'Language: Arabic dialect predominates'*- Another *'specific attribute'* could be better addressed here too, *'Arabic limited/French limited'*. Both of these attributes do refer to the same wider linguistic vision:

- The *'key issue'* shown (**Column.3**) both attributes is *'Culture'*: in the <u>first case</u>, it is moderate with a two (2) stars rating and in <u>the second</u>, it is weak with one (1) star rating. You might perceive this to be completely different, this is totally acceptable, just justify your answers.

- The SWOT contributions, in both cases, are depicted in (**Column.4**):

In case-1, the Arabic dialect: this may be an <u>*opportunity*</u> that we can explore, as far as the social side is concerned.

In case-2, however, people coming out from universities not mastering neither the Arabic Language nor the French is a definite <u>*Weakness*</u> and could even be perceived as a threat. How do you, yourself, view this analysis?

Our fourth perspective of the PESTLE model is 'technical' (Table.2, lower part).

The first '*specific attribute*' in this part of the '***technical***' analysis is: '*ICT good standard: DSL, fibre optic, Computers*' **Column.2)**: Algeria ICT (Information and Communication Technology) is of a reasonable standard, but in a lot of aspects as we will see later.

- The '*key issue*' shown (**Column.3**) is '*ICT*' with a two (2) stars rating: moderate.

- The SWOT perspective, (**Column.4**), views this only as an '*Opportunity*', there is more to do, and more that can be done (see next).

With regard to the next '*specific attribute*' (**Colimn.2**): '*Internet: low penetration*':

- As an ICT '*key issue*' (**Column.3**) this carries a one (1) star rating: weak, and,

- The SWOT perspective, (**Column.4**), perceives to be a 'Weakness, even a Threat'

From both angles, this tells us that the *Internet low penetration* is a poor ICT sign and worse; particularly under the umbrella of the '*technical*' perspective (of the PESTLE Analysis).

The next '*specific attribute*' addressed is: *Mobile telephony: widespread* (**Column.2**):

- The '*key issue*' shown (**Column.3**) is still '*ICT*' with a one (1) star rating: weak.

- From a SWOT perspective, (**Column.4**), there is an '*Opportunity*'. You may consider the matter under a more positive light for other reasons than the following:

- From the ICT point of view only, '*Mobile Telephony widespread*' is a good thing, which is not reflected by the rating of one (1) star because this is not going to take the country very far considering that the *Internet is low penetration*. On the other hand, there is an opportunity to explore here, as far as the SWOT model is concerned.

(**Column.2**) identifies the next '*specific attribute*' to be: *computer illiteracy, high* '.

- The '*key issue*' shown (**Column.3**) being '*ICT*' with a two (2) stars rating: moderate,

- How about the SWOT insights into the analysis? (**Column.4**) shows this to be a *Weakness*. This is very true, considering that, nowadays '*computer illiteracy*' is illiteracy in the full meaning of the word', and this can only be a '*Weakness*'.

Our fifth perspective of the PESTLE model is 'legal' (Table.3).

Table.3: PESTLE Analysis, 'Case Study-1: Algeria, Part.3'

\multicolumn{4}{c}{**The PESTLE Analysis: Case Study 'Algeria'**}			
PESTLE	**Background (Specific attributes)**	*Algeria EC Key Issues*	**S.W.O.T**
L- Legal	- Legislate, Regulate Environment of EC	- *Legislation (legal)* [***]	- Threats
	- EC, only Register of Commerce number attributed	- *Legislation (legal)* [**]	- Opportunity
	- e-tailing/ e-banking: No legislation in place	- *Legislation (legal)* [***]	- Weakness
E- Environ mental	As above, with the following specific points:		
	- Climate: Only 2 seasons (Summer / Winter)	- *e-Trade* [**]	- Weakness
	- Pollution in big towns	- *e-Trade* [**]	- Threat
	- Poor Railway infrastructure, more cars on the Road: noise, pollution, accidents	- *CRM* [*]	- Threat
	- Clean Air in Small towns & Rural Areas	- *e-Trade*	- Opportunity
	- Agriculture: was predominant, not much now	-*e-Trade*	- Weakness
	- Oil& Gas: predominate in the Sahara	-*e-Trade*	- Opportunity
	- Sahara: drought, sandstorms,	- *e-payment (e-banking)* [*]	- Weak / Threat.
	- Sahara: rich in palm trees & quality dates	- *e-Marketing* [*]	- Opportunity
Keys:	[*]=Weak ; [**]: Moderate; [***]: Strong		

| EC Key Issues | e-Government, e-Trade, CRM, e-payment (e-banking), e-Marketing, Human Resources, Social Networks, Culture, ICT, Legislation (legal), |

The first '*specific attribute*' in this part of the '*legal*' analysis is: '*Legislate, Regulate Environment of EC*' (**Column.2**):

- The '*key issue*' shown (**Column.3**) is '*Legislation*' with a three (3) stars rating: strong. The legislation is central here to the e-Commerce dimension.

- The SWOT perspective, (**Column.4**), views this as 'Threat' that underlines the importance of the '*legislation*'. Particularly in the EC (e-Commerce) industry, which is key in this analysis, and is missing altogether, non-existent?

The next '*specific attribute*' to address is: '*EC, only Register of Commerce Number attributed*' (**Column.2**):

- The '*key issue*' shown (**Column.3**) is '*Legislation*' with a two (2) stars rating: moderate. People wouldn't know what to do, as far as the legal side of it is concerned, and in the e-commerce industry, particularly. For e-commerce, '*only a register of commerce number is attributed*' to the enterprise concerned: moderate.

- The SWOT perspective, (**Column.4**), views this as an '*Opportunity*', particularly in this brand new field of EC (e-Commerce), where legislation is non-existent. This first attempt is an Opportunity because that may develop and enable the e-commerce business to take off.

The next '*specific attribute*' addressed is: '*e-tailing and e-banking*' (**Column.2**):

- The '*key issue*' shown (**Column.3**) is '*Legislation*' with a three (3) stars rating: strong.

- From a SWOT perspective, (**Column.4**), this is a Weakness situation: no *legislation* in place for such an important '*key issue*' (a strong one).

N.B: See how you may develop this part and the next one further: their analysis here will be much lighter leaving you room to enrich it.

The next '*specific attribute*' being considered is: '*climate: only two seasons, summer and winter*' (**Column.2**):

- The '*key issue*' shown (**Column.3**) is '*e-trade*' with a two (2) stars rating: moderate. Why such a rating, from your point of view.

- From a SWOT perspective, (**Column.4**), we are dealing with a Weakness situation. Do you agree with that? If not, why not. If you do, why?

    You might see that there is here an Opportunity (with the two seasons) that could be explored.

(**Column.2**) identifies the next '*specific attribute*' as being: '*pollution in big towns*:

- The '*key issue*' shown (**Column.3**) is '*e-trade*' with a two (2) stars rating: moderate. In your opinion does the *e-trade* suffer from the '*pollution in big towns*'? If so, why? if not why not. Does this justify a moderate 2-stars rating?

- From a SWOT perspective, (**Column.4**), we are dealing with a *Threat* situation. You could say that all big towns in the world are polluted, but isn't pollution a threat? Do you agree with there being a *Threat* here? If not, why not. If so, why?

The next '*specific attribute*' is: '*poor railway infrastructure, more cars on the road: noise, pollution, accidents*' (**Column.2**):

- The '*key issue*' shown (**Column.3**) is '*e-trade*' with a two (2) stars rating: moderate. If you agree, show your analysis of the matter. If not, why not?

- The SWOT perspective, (**Column.4**), interprets the overall situation as a *Threat*. Doesn't that contradict the moderate rating above?

The following '*specific attributes*' shown by (**Column.2**) are:

1) '*Clean air in small towns*'
2) '*Agriculture was predominant, not so much now*'
3) ' *Oil and Gas predominate in the Sahara*
4) ' *Sahara: drought, sandstorms*
5) ' *Sahara: rich in palm trees and quality dates*'

- The related '*key issues*' to the above '*specific attributes*' are shown in (**Column.3**),
- **Column.4**) depicts each of the relevant SWOT perspectives.

Exercise: Fill in the table below with what your own assessment should be, as far as:

- the 'key issues' are concerned (in your opinion)
- the 'SWOT' insights are concerned (in your opinion)

PESTLE Perspective	Specific Attribute	Key Issue	SWOT Perspective
Environmental	1-'*Clean air in small towns*'		
	2-*Agriculture was predominant, not so much now*		
	3-*Oil and Gas predominate in the Sahara*		
	4 *Sahara: drought, sandstorms*		
	5 *Sahara: rich in palm trees and quality dates*		

We have attempted to cover the PESTLE Analysis from all its six perspectives. We have carried out a PESTLE Analysis that gives you a way of actually taking the theory, taking the fundamentals of the PESTLE Analysis and applying them in a real situation.

What you are advised to do, at this stage, are to consider your own company or your country, and attempt to apply the PESTLE Analysis to it, so that you get as close to the realities of the analysis as possible. As you can see the PESTLE Analysis is a very comprehensive analytical method that you can use in every possible situation that is.

12. CONCLUSION OF THE SECTION

The PESTLE Analysis: 'Conclusion'

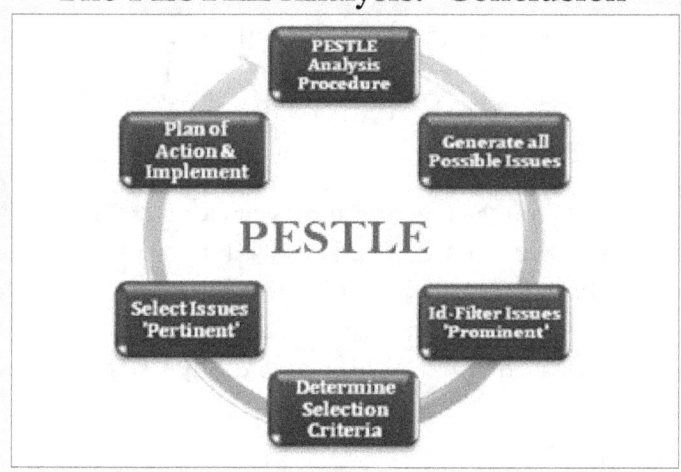

Figure.20: PESTLE Analysis2, Conclusion

Having carried out an analysis using the PESTLE model on the case study of Algeria, we are now going to close this chapter through this conclusion (**Figure.20**). What follows is a refresher a recap on what we have covered so far.

We have identified that the objective of the PESTLE Analysis may vary according to the focus of the analysis itself. The analysis that we have carried out on the case study of Algeria was from its e-commerce angle.

Where the focus was on 'environmental', for example, we used the analysis to identify how external key trends impact on a department, a company, an organization, or even a nation, as we've done about Algeria.

The model requires that the Analyst carries out the analysis of the entity under study, in light of each of the six elements (the six dimensions), in order to determine risks, raise issues, identify opportunities and so on. That's exactly what we've done in those tables, in the last column, via the SWOT analysis.

PESTLE, why should we consider using it? We do because it focuses on the external factors and their impact on the organization itself. It is a strategic planning tool that focuses on these outside factors, and how they influence the business itself.

The PESTLE Analysis is used to provide insights into these factors and it measures their impact. As such, it concentrates essentially on the macro environment of the organization. When we say *organization*, bear in mind that this could well be a department or a nation as we have done in the case study of Algeria.

As such, this concentrates essentially on the macro environment of the organization and enables Analysts to develop insights into the organization and their study.

PESTLE is a framework; it's a framework to attempt to analyze key external factors that determine a considerable impact on most organizations; a framework that attempts to focus on the level of competition within the industry of the organizations under study.

It, therefore, looks at the environment of the organization with a view of getting better insights on what happens inside the organization under study.

It is often perceived as the ideal tool for strategic analysis, driven by these different outside factors that impact the business: Political, Economic Social, Technical, Legal and Environmental, as we have seen through the last case study of Algeria.

These varieties of the model include PESTLE, PESTEL, PEST, etc. These are different ways versions of the same thing and we can use them interchangeably, depending on what we intend to achieve from the study itself. They share, however, the common purpose of analyzing the key trends that impact the organization's outside system, its external environment, but on which the organization bears no influence.

In a way the above analogy is like a system: if you are inside the system you are influenced by its environment. But, as an organization within this system, you cannot directly impact on the environment that surrounds you.

The PESTLE Analysis seeks to focus on those key trends that impact the department, the company, the organization or nation from the six PESTLE angles. The focus needs to be on trends and on quantifying the impact, as we have done, for example, by using the (stars) rating that we have adopted through the case study analysis

The PESTLE Analysis is often used in conjunction with other analytical methods, such as the CAGE analysis, the Porter's Five Forces analysis, or the SWOT analysis, as we have outlined in the practice exercise.

In the latter case, we have seen that PESTLE factors can be classified as Opportunities or Threats by the SWOT analysis, which is commonly used in pairs with the PESTLE model. It is often useful to complete the PESTLE Analysis before completing the SWOT analysis. At times, it is better to do them simultaneously, as we have done in our practice case study.

ANNEX-A:

'PESTLE' ANALYSIS APPLIED TO ALGERIA E-COMMERCE

Table.4: Annex-A, PESTLE Analysis 'Global Case Study'

PESTLE	Background (Specific attributes)	*Algeria EC Key Issues*	S.W.O.T
P-Political	- A black decade (of terrorism) impacted politics	- *e-Government [***]*	- Threat
	- Country moved from Socialist to Capitalist	- *e-Government [**]*	- Opportunity
	- Democracy: at the infancy stage	- *e-Government [*]*	- Opportunity
	- Corruption heavy, and at various levels (see social)	- *e-Government [**]*	- Weakness/ Threat
E-Economic	As above, with the following specific points:		
	- Country: Developing	- *e-Trade[***]*	- Opportunity
	- Public companies dominate market vs. Private	- *e-Trade[*]*	- Weakness
	- CRM culture poor (see Social)	- *CRM/ e-Marketing[**]*	- Threat
	- Banking system inefficient/ e-banking missing	- *e-Trade[**]*	- Threat
	- SCM (logistics most inefficient, when existing)	- *e-Trade[**]*	- Weaknesses
	- Currency: Algerian Dinar, not convertible	- *e-banking/ e-banking[*]*	- Weakness
	- Inflation: officially declared around 3%, in reality in double figures	- *e-Trade[**]*	- Threat
S-Social	- A 'black decade' (of terrorism) affected Algeria	- *Human Resources [***]*	- Threat
	- Corruption heavy, and at various levels	- *Human*	- Threat

	- Culture (Islam) strong, but with minor resistance	Resources [**] - Human Resources [*]	- Opportunity - Threat
	- Illiteracy very high indeed: up-to 11 Million	- Social Networks[***]	- Opportunity
	- Language: Arabic Dialect (Arabic) predominates/ - Arabic: limited /French: limited	- Culture [**] - Culture [*]	- Weaknesses/ Threat
T- Technical	- ICT, good standard: DSL, Fiber optic, Computers	- ICT [**]	- Opportunity
	- Internet: low penetration	- ICT [*]	- Weakn's/ Threats
	- Mobile Telephony: widespread	- ICT[*]	- Opportunity
	- Computer illiteracy, high	- ICT[**]	- Weakness
L- Legal	- Legislate, Regulate Environment of EC	- Legislation (legal) [***]	- Threats
	- EC, only Register of Commerce number attributed	- Legislation (legal) [**]	- Opportunity
	- e-tailing/ e-banking: No legislation in place	- Legislation (legal) [***]	- Weakness
E- Environm ental	**As above, with the following specific points:**		
	- Climate: Only 2 seasons (Summer/Winter)	- e-Trade[**]	- Weakness
	- Pollution in big towns	- e-Trade[**]	- Threat
	- Poor Railway infrastructure, more cars on the Road: noise, pollution, accidents	- e-Trade[**]	- Threat
	- Clean Air in Small towns & Rural Areas	- CRM[*]	- Opportunity
	- Agriculture: was predominant, not so much	- e-Trade	- Weakness

	now		
	- Oil& Gas: predominate in the Sahara	-e-Trade	- Opportunity
	- Sahara: drought, sandstorms,	-e-Trade	- Weaknesses/ Threat
	- Sahara: rich in palm trees & quality dates	- e-payment (e-banking) [*] - e-Marketing [*]	- Opportunity
Keys:	[*]=Weak ; [**]: Moderate; [***]: Strong		
EC Key Issues	e-Government, e-Trade, CRM, e-payment (e-banking), e-Marketing, Human Resources, Social Networks, Culture, ICT, Legislation (legal),		

SECTION II

BUSINESS ANALYSIS TOOLS APPLIED: 'THE CAGE FRAMEWORK'

Objective:

Architecture, Perspective and Application of the CAGE Four Dimensions: Cultural, Administrative, Geographic, Economic

EXECUTIVE SUMMARY: THE 'CAGE'

This Section will enable the Readers to master the CAGE Framework, a powerful Business Analysis Tool. It will further empower their Problem Solving and Decision Making.

As a Reader, you will learn the Business Strategic Analysis fundamentals and Apply them through the C.A.G.E framework. CAGE being acronym for: Cultural, Administrative, Geographic and Economic. These CAGE's four Perspectives make it a thorough Business Strategic Analysis Tool.

Readers, with a need or keen interest for Business Analysis or Strategic Business Analysis and those who want to learn and apply the powerful CAGE Analysis tool to their enterprise (or that of their clients), will learn some powerful skills in the process.

What you'll learn

- You will learn the Business Strategic Analysis fundamentals and how to apply them through the C.A.G.E framework's four Dimensions above.
- You will learn such fundamentals of Strategic Business Analysis through examples and case studies first and then through a Project: a practice section which will teach you how you can apply the CAGE model as a Tool in real-life Business analysis situations.

- Readers who will benefit strongly from this book are those with keen interest in Business Analysis, Problem Solving and rigorous Decision Making and those who want to learn and apply the powerful CAGE Analysis tool to study their enterprise or that of their clients.

THE CAGE - INTRODUCTION

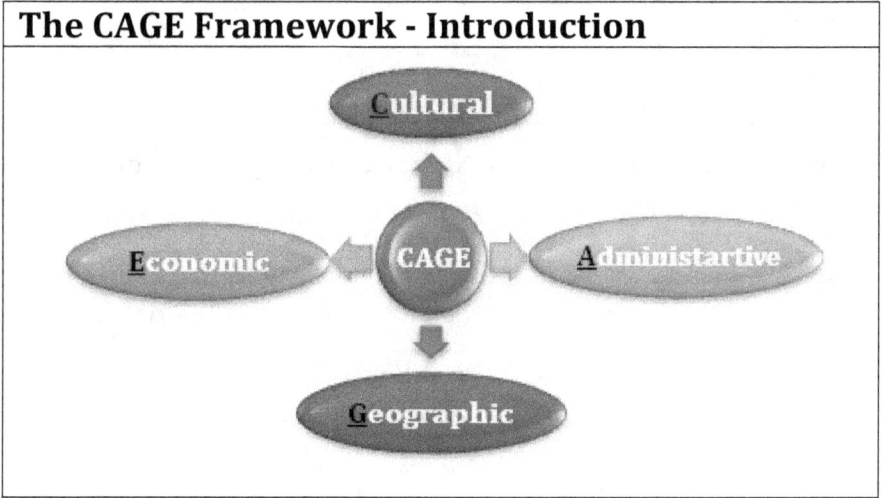

Figure.1: The CAGE, Introduction

This section is about the CAGE framework. **(Figure.1)** is a visual representation of this.

In short, the CAGE framework is used to identify the *distance* of the organization *under study* from its *desirable situation*: how far it is from its desired destination.

Consider the diagrammatic representation of (**Figure.2**). We have at one end, the *'entity under study'* (what_is) and at the other end its *'desirable situation'*. (To_be) and the *distance* between them. This distance between where we are and where we want to be is expressed in terms of **C**ultural, **A**dministrative, **G**eographic and **E**conomic, which spell C.A.G.E. They are the four perspectives of the CAGE model and that's what the framework of the model helps us to determine.

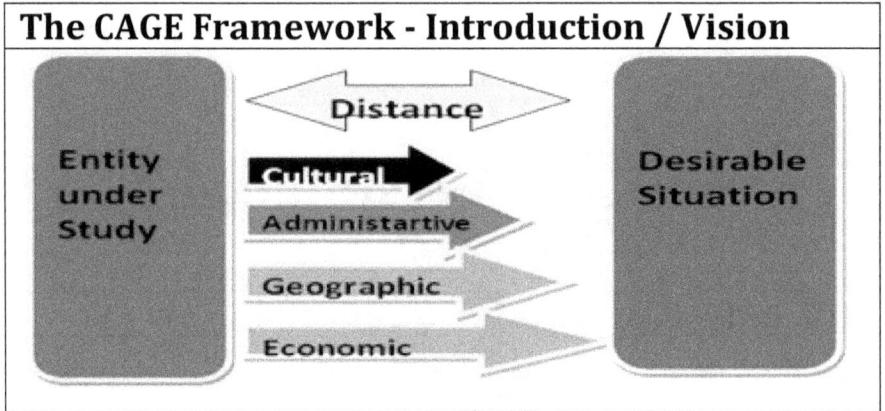

Figure.2: The CAGE Introduction, Model Representation

In fact, the model goes even further and enable us to assess the *impact of this distance* on each of the four perspective / elements. The impact can be negative or it can be positive. Let's look at this through an example:

Consider DeBeers, a famous diamonds leader. DeBeers want to set up a business in China. So, they have chosen the CAGE framework to study the situation they are in, as famous diamond leaders in Europe, and the desirable situation to set up another business in China: the situation between what / where they are and the situation where they want to be.

There is here a distance, no doubt, and they want to look at this distance from four different points of view: Cultural, Administrative, Geographical, Economical (**Figure.2a**).They want to look at the distance. in each case. and determine what / where they are and what they want to be. So, the CAGE framework would be an ideal tool for them to use. We want to start looking at the analysis at this stage because it would serve our purpose in our project, later on.

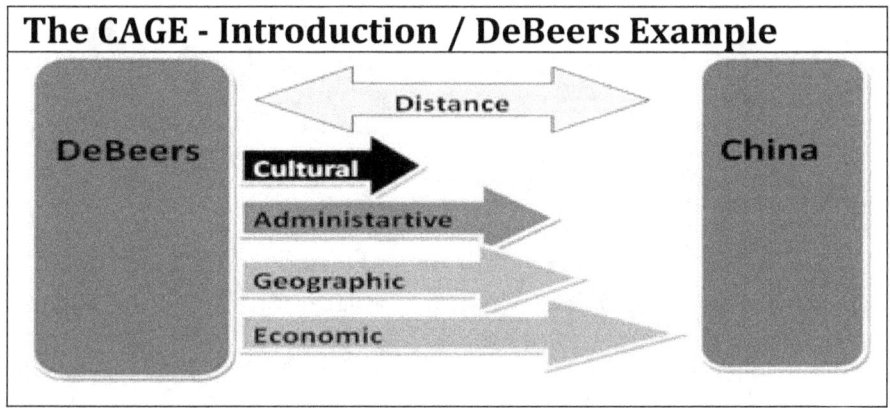

Figure.2a: The CAGE Introduction, DeBeers Example

For now, let's get a feel of how DeBeers' Analyst would approach this situation.

- He may consider, as a choice, to carry out the analysis as to why, from a strategic perspective, DeBeers would go to China.

- He may tackle this initially from an 'A*dministrative* & *Political*' distance and determine what this 'distance' is (**Figure.2b**) and decide whether it is of a positive or negative impact.

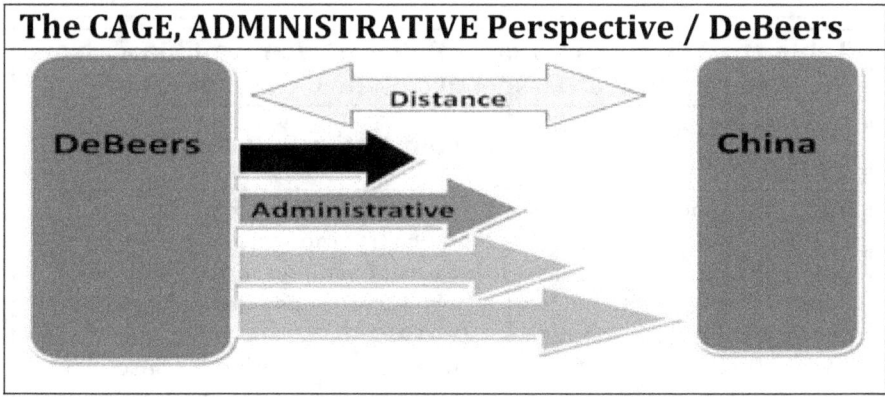

Figure.2b: The CAGE, DeBeers - Administrative Dimension

- Practically, he could set up a two-columns table as shown by (**Table.1**),

- He would consider, for instance, the bottom element of the table; "*Does the distance affect most of the diamond industry in China?* (**Column.1**);

- He would review this element in light of the *Administrative & Political* distance and identify all its related items, item by item (**Column.2**);

- He would determine in each case if the item is of a positive (**+ve**) or negative (**-ve**) impact. For instance:

*1- In light of the Administrative & Political distance, the first item (**Column.2**), which is "shared monetary or political association, none", has a (**-ve**) impact; which means that the distance in this respect is greater (the item is problematic): as indicated at the top of (**Column.1**).*

*2- The second item (**Column.2**), "Political hostilities, none", has a (**+ve**) impact; which means that the distance in this respect is smaller (the item is not so much of a problem): as indicated at the top of (**Column.1**).*

Table.1: The CAGE Analysis, Example: DeBeers Case Study

The CAGE - Introduction / DeBeers Case Study-1	
Table.1: CAGE Analysis of " DeBeers went to China", from the 'Administrative' perspective of the CAGE Framework.	
[-ve]=negative [+ve]=positive	**Administrative & (Political Distance)**
The Distance between DeBeers and China (as potential host) increases when the aspect under consideration is marked: [-ve]	* Shared monetary or political association, none: [-ve] * Political hostilities, none [+ve] * Legal Institutions tight and opening [+/-ve]; * financial institutions consolidating their base and improving [+ve]
Does the Distance affect most the diamond industry in China?	*China Government does not view as staples, building national reputation nor as vital to national security: [+ve]

These steps will hopefully help you build your starting approach to the analysis and will lead you to focus your study on how you could go from a concept to a real life situation. For now, just get a feel for what the CAGE analysis may offer.

(Annex-A) will provide you with all the necessary tables - such as - (**Table.1**) to enable you to follow the analysis and they will serve a great purpose later on when you do your project on DeBeers.

1. THE CAGE - CULTURAL DIMENSION

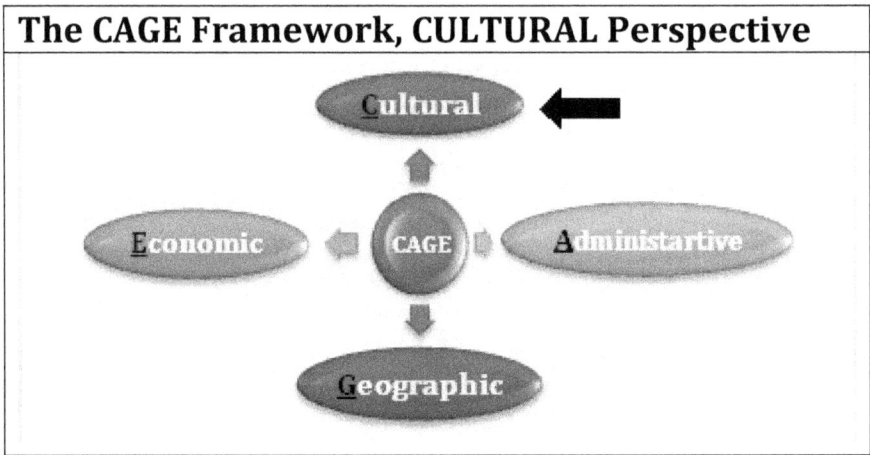

Figure.3: The CAGE, Cultural Dimension - Context

Consider now the CAGE framework's first perspective, the *Cultural* perspective / dimension. (**Figure.3**) provides a visual representation so that we know, at all times, where we are going and what we want to achieve.

The example below relates to DeBeers, which we have introduced earlier on. We are using DeBeers example, because it is a practical case study. Also, we are basing our practical approach on the four perspectives of the CAGE model.

Example (Case Study):

As a case in hand, let's look at the diamond industry in China again and draw some conclusions, this time, from a cultural perspective, as to why DeBeers (leader's in the diamond industry) went to China..

Through this example, we will look at the *diamond industry* in China and draw some conclusions, from a *cultural* perspective, as to why DeBeers, who are leaders in the diamond industry, went to China.

We have seen the global approach as represented by the visual diagram (**Figure.2**), and now let us focus on one particular aspect of that diagram (of the CAGE framework), the *Culture* perspective and use DeBeers' case study for the analysis (**Figure.4**).

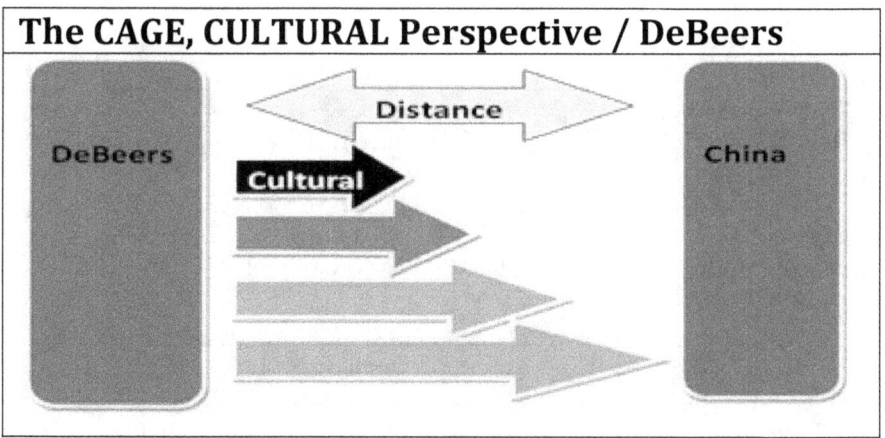

Figure.4: The CAGE, DeBeers - Cultural Dimension

(**Figure.4**) shows the box '*DeBeers*' as the situation which they are in (**As_is**), the box '*China*' as the situation they want to be in (**To_be**), and the *distance* between the two: how far they are from their goal. They want to consider, first of all, this *distance* from a *Culture* dimension.

In the same way as initiated above (**Table.1**), we build a '*culture*' oriented table (**Table.2**). Note that the practice section adopts this very style and approach and (**Annex-A**) groups these different perspectives tables.

(**Table.2**) looks at the *impact* of the *cultural* dimension of the CAGE framework. It identifies whether it's positive (+ve) or negative (-ve). The distance between *DeBeers* and *China* (as potential host) increases when the aspect under consideration is market negative (-ve). Put simply, this signifies: longer distance, (-ve) aspect because there is here a longer way to reach the desirable destination.

Table.2: The CAGE Analysis - Cultural Perspective

The CAGE, CULTURAL Perspective / DeBeers Case Study-1	
Table-1a ------------------------- [-ve]=negative [+ve]=positive	**Cultural (Distance)**
The Distance between DeBeers and China (as potential host) increases when the aspect under consideration is marked: [-ve]	* **Differences in** : - China's Culture from that in most Parts of the World where DeBeers operates:[-ve] - Ethnicities too, [-ve] - Religion and Social norms [-ve] * Lack Connective ethnic or social networks: [-ve]
Does the Distance affect most the diamond industry in China?	* Not high Linguistic content [+ve] * Not related to Chinese Identity[+ve] * Not carrying country-specific quality association: [+ve}

Different 'cultural' aspects are identified under '*Differences in:*' (**Column2**). A (-ve) rating signifies a wider gap before, a problematic aspect :

1- "*China's culture from that in most parts of the world where DeBeers operates, negative*": (-ve);

2- "*ethnicities too, negative*" (-ve);
3- "*Religion and social norms, negative*" (-ve)

Let's just develop this capacity of passing from the *conceptual* diagram on to the *application*, as done by an Analyst. We will develop this approach progressively until we build a kind of a guide which the Analyst would go through.

2. THE CAGE - ADMINISTRATIVE DIMENSION

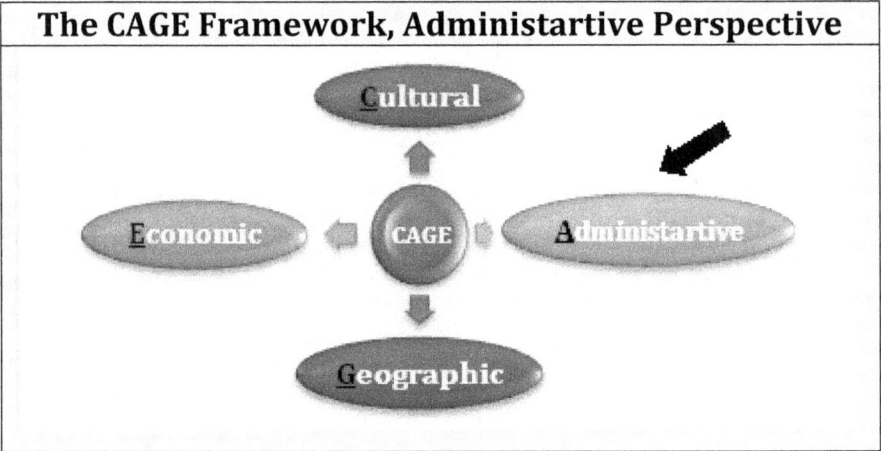

Figure.5: The CAGE, Administrative Dimension

Let us now focus on the *Administrative* dimension / perspective of the CAGE framework. It is the *Administrative* dimension with the *Political* "flavour". We will still maintain our DeBeers case study and our analysis approach using the CAGE model. We will look at the diamond industry and draw conclusions - this time, from the *Administrative & Political* distance - as to why, from a strategic perspective, DeBeers (who are leaders in the diamond industry) went to China. What does that tell us?

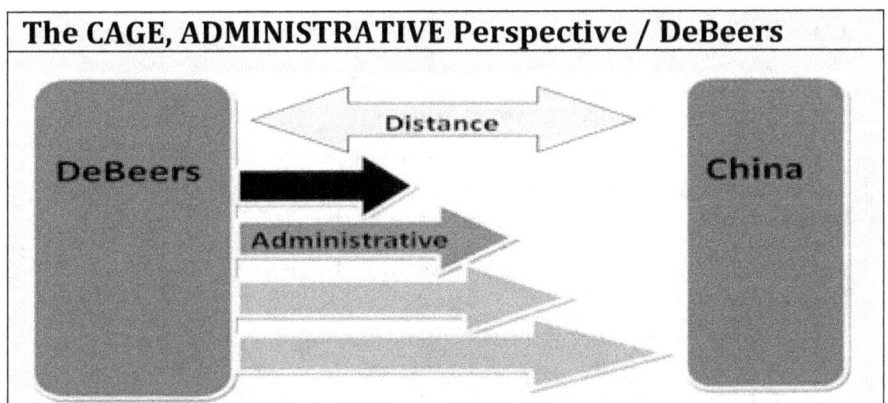

Figure.6: The CAGE, Administrative dimension - study

(**Figure.6**) shows a visual diagram that we have got to keep in mind for the analysis. DeBeers wants to go and set up a business in China and they are using the CAGE framework to analyze the situation and determine the *distance* there is between where they are (**As_is**) and the desirable situation (**To_be**) from an *Administrative* point of view, as opposed to a *cultural* point of view (considered above). Our analysis seeks to determine also if that *distance* has any negative (**-ve**) impact or a positive (**+ve**) impact on DeBeers objective: setting up business in China.

Let's see how this conceptual diagram (**Figure.6**) is going to be translated by an Analyst into a *data format*, a table. There is a table that we can build (**Table.3**). As you can see the table is now called *Administrative* perspective of the CAGE framework.

As a reminder, note (top of **Colum.1**) the qualifiers: negative (**-ve**) and positive (**+ve**) which relate to the *impact* that an item relating to the *Administrative* aspect (in **Column.2**) has on DeBeers moving to China.

We are slowly gaining experience in our analysis approach using the CAGE model. Let us look now consider (**Column.2**) from an *Administrative* point of view. What has changed in this table by comparison to (**Table.1**)?

Table.3: The CAGE Analysis - Administrative Perspective

The CAGE, ADMINISTRATIVE Perspective / DeBeers Case Study-2	
Table.1b: CAGE Analysis of " DeBeers went to China", from the 'Administrative' perspective of the CAGE Framework.	
[-ve]=negative [+ve]=positive	Administrative & (Political Distance)
The Distance between DeBeers and China (as potential host) increases when the aspect under consideration is marked: [-ve]	* Shared monetary or political association, none: [-ve] * Political hostilities, none [+ve] * Legal Institutions tight and opening[+/-ve]; * financial institutions consolidating their base and improving [+ve]
Does the Distance affect most the diamond industry in China?	* China Government does not view as staples, building national reputation nor as vital to national security: [+ve]

In fact, all the items now relate to the *'Administrative'* dimension (as opposed to *'Cultural'* - seen before):

1- "*shared monetary or political association, none*", *negative* (-ve): this means that the *distance* is bigger for DeBeers with a view to setting up business in China.

2- "*political hostilities, none*" (+ve): no political hostilities indicates that the *distance* here is smaller, that this a positive impact for DeBeers moving to China.

3- "*legal institutions tight and opening*" *(+ve / -ve)*: this indicates that the impact can be positive (+ve) or be negative (-ve) a (50/50 situation).

4- "*financial institutions in China consolidating their base and improving*" *positive (+ve): a* shorter *distance*, a definite positive impact here on DeBeers objective.

5- *China Government does not view as staples, building national reputation nor as vital to national security"(+ve)*: again, in this case the *distance* for DeBeers is smaller and the *impact* is thus positive (+ve).

Note: let's remember that if the impact is negative (-ve) that means the *distance* is bigger, which means it is impacting negatively on the idea of DeBeers going to China. If it is positive that means the *distance* is shorter.

By now we are hopefully getting more familiar with this progress from a *conceptual diagram* to building a *data format (table)*, to facilitate the CAGE analysis, under each of its four dimensions.

3. THE CAGE - GEOGRAPHIC DIMENSION

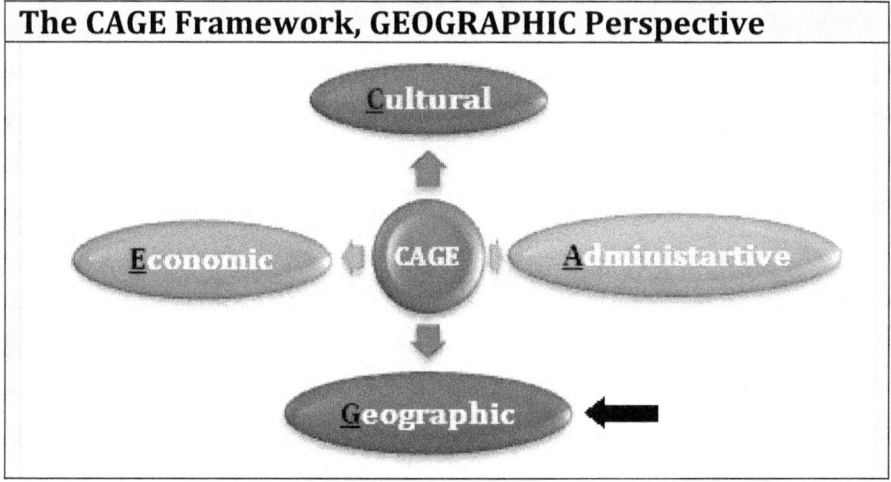

Figure.7: The CAGE, Geographic Dimension - Context

Let us now look at the CAGE framework, this time from its third dimension, the *Geographic* perspective. (**Figure.7**) provides a visual representation of the CAGE framework which helps us keep the overall picture in mind.

So, we have covered thus far the *Cultural*, the *Administrative* and now we are looking at the *Geographic* dimension of the CAGE framework.

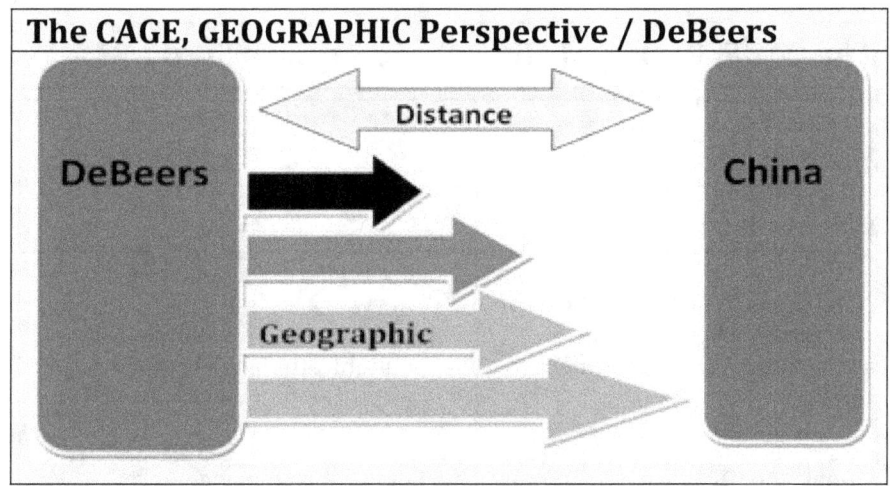

Figure.8: The CAGE, Geographic Dimension -Study

Along the same approach developed earlier, we consider our same case study and look at the diamond industry in China, with regard to DeBeers, but from a *Geographic* perspective.

In short, we will look at the *distance*, for DeBeers to move to China, from a *Geographic* perspective, seeking to determine the *impact* that this has over such move (**Figure.8**). Being more familiar with the procedure by now, we shall proceed much quicker through the coming analysis.

So, let us develop this and start by looking at how our concept above translates, once again, into a data format (**Table.4**).

We are familiar with the terminology and know what the *distance* implies, when it is positive (+ve) or negative (-ve), in terms of *impact* on DeBeers moving to China.

Table.4: The CAGE Analysis - Geographic Perspective

The CAGE, GEOGRAPHIC / DeBeers Case Study-3	
Table-1c --------------------------------- [-ve] = negative / [+ve] = positive	**Geographic (Distance)**
The Distance between DeBeers and China (as potential host) increases when the aspect under consideration is marked: [-ve]	* Common borders, none [-ve] * Waterway access [+ve] * Adequate transportation [+ve] * Communication Links [+ve] * Physical remoteness: far [-ve] * Climate, good [+ve]
Does the Distance affect most the diamond industry in China?	* High value-to-low weight ratio [+ve] * Not Fragile nor perishable [+ve] but too precious [-ve] * in which communications are vital [+/-ve]

So, we ask ourselves *"Does the distance affect most the diamond industry in China?"* (bottom, **Column.1**), and seek to get some answers, from a *Geographic* perspective **(Column.2)**:

1- *"high value-to-low weight ratio, positive (+ve)"*. This is positive, which indicates that the impact here (on DeBeers objective) is positive.

2- *"(diamonds) not fragile nor perishable (+ve), but too precious (-ve)"*. This impact relating here to the goods is, in the first part, positive (goods travel well) and in the second part negative (goods carry a greater risk), from a *Geographic* perspective. You may want to deepen this analysis further, if you so wish and derive a different conclusion.

3- *"in which communications are vital,* **(+ve / -ve)***"*. Depending on your interpretation 'communications are vital' could be positive or negative, because when communications are vital, this can make them vital for better or for worse. How would address this element?

Now let us as ask some of the questions here (top **Colum.2**) and see them in the light of the *Geographic* dimension of the CAGE framework. At the same time, we need to keep an eye on the *impact* they have on DeBeers analysis, with a view of setting up a business in China:

5- "*common borders, none (-ve)*": there aren't any common borders (DeBeers main base is Europe) so this particular *distance* is negative.

6- "*waterway access, (+ve)*": the *distance* here (and thus the impact) is positive, for DeBeers move, from a *geographic* perspective, because boats can go easily from Europe to China.

7- "*adequate transportation (+ve)*": there is here another positive aspect (*distance & impact*) for De Beers, because flights as well boat trips to and from China are abundant.

8- "*Communication links, (+ve)*": the communication network and infrastructure to and from China is considerable. The distance here for DeBeers (in light of the geographic perspective) is positive.

9- "*Physical remoteness, (-ve)*": China is in Asia, far from Europe's (DeBeers) continent, this makes physical remoteness a negative aspect, for DeBeers' move: the distance is bigger and the impact is therefore negative. Do you agree with this analysis? Do you interpret "remoteness" otherwise?

10- What about "*the climate is good*"?: good climate can only help matters and, consequently, this makes the **distance** shorter and the *impact* positive, for DeBeers move to China, from a *Geographic* perspective

The above steps should provide you with a succinct guide which enables to launch a CAGE analysis. In addition, it should help you transpose your idea, from a concept, to a data format suitable to base the analysis on, as we have experienced so far. What has been carried out under the *Geographic* dimension of the CAGE model is equally applicable for the last dimension, the economic one.

4. THE CAGE - ECONOMIC DIMENSION

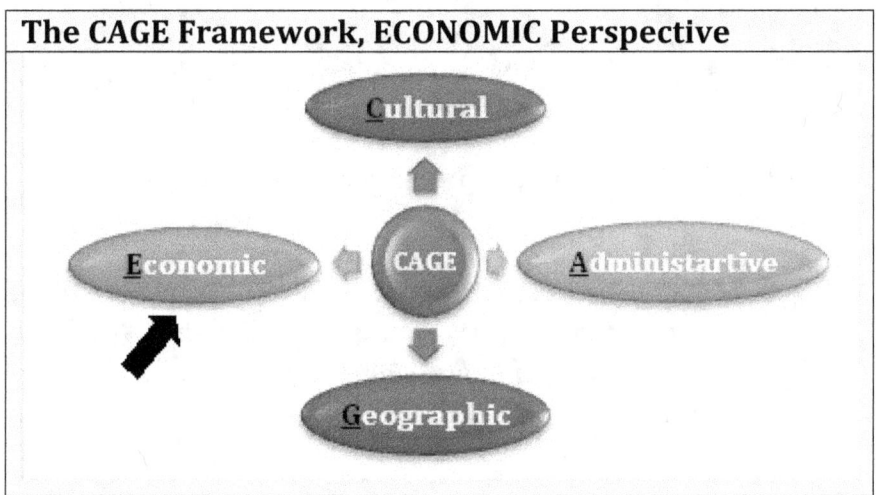

Figure.9: The CAGE, Economic Dimension - Context

This is the last dimension of the CAGE framework, the E*conomic* perspective. (**Figure.9**) provides the visual representation of the framework. It shows the perspectives which we have covered thus far: Cultural, Administrative and Geographic perspectives, as well as the Economic one, yet to address.

You are by now used to the method and the terminology and it should be even easier if we used the same case study of 'DeBeers going to China'. So, let's launch the analysis of the latter, this time from the '*Economic*' perspective of the CAGE model.

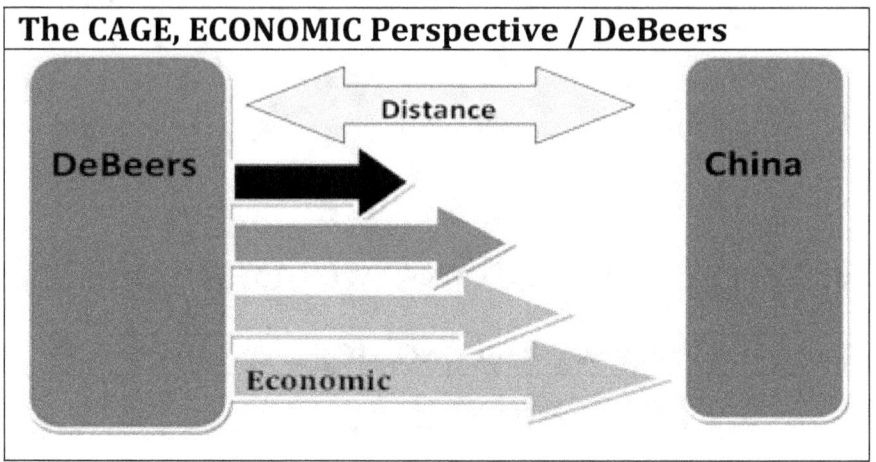

Figure.10: The CAGE, Economic Dimension - Study

Consider (**Figure.10**); it is a virtual representation of the CAGE framework that shows the two entities '*DeBeers*' going to '*China*', with the '***Economic***' *distance* being analyzed. We seek to determine the *impact* which that *distance* has on the project of DeBeers to move part of their business to China.

Let's see how this visual representation of the CAGE framework, the '*Economics*' perspective, can be translated into a data format, for the purpose of our analysis. How can this be translated, later on, into a report by the Analyst, a report to the customer in an understandable format?

(**Table.5**) is the data format sought. As a matter of interest, this table is included within the set of four in (**Annex-A**). Together they will serve the purpose of a practice session, a project session, which will be initiated at the end of this section.

Moreover, some notes are provided in (**Annex-A, Resources**). They are related to DeBeers moving to China. It might be a good idea to familiarize yourself with this annex at this stage. You may want to leave it till the end and tackle it all at the *project stage*.

As you are used to the process used in the analysis depicted by (**Table.5**), we will only focus on the essentials., starting with the element:

Table.5: The CAGE Analysis - Economic Perspective

The CAGE, ECONOMIC / DeBeers Case Study-4	
Table-1d -------------------------------- [-ve] = negative / [+ve] = positive	Economic (Distance)
The Distance between DeBeers and China (as potential host) increases when the aspect under consideration is marked: [-ve]	* Consumer Incomes: fast rising middle class: [+ve] * Costs and quality of natural, financial & human resources [+ve] * Information Knowledge [+ve]
Does the Distance affect most the diamond industry in China?	* diamond demand varies according to income: bigger purse, bigger diamond[-ve] * In diamonds labor and cost differences matter [+/-ve]

"*Does the distance affect most of the diamond industry in China?*" (bottom of **Column.1**).

Let's look at this, in light of the ***Economic*** perspective, reference (bottom part of **Column.2**):

1- "*Diamond demand varies according to income: bigger purse, bigger diamond, (-ve)*": Is that the case in China? Not quite! That will be a negative *distance* and that will have a negative *impact* on the vision that DeBeers want to establish about going to China. Do you agree? if so why? if not, why not? Try and develop this further ready for the practice session.

2- "*in diamonds labour and cost differences matter (+ve / -ve):* how is that going to *impact* on DeBeers going to China? We don't quite know. So the *distance* may be bigger or smaller and the impact on DeBeers' goal could swing either way. This is represented by *(+ve / -ve)*. How do you interpret this case yourself?

Let us now consider some particular points of importance for DeBeers moving to China, under the *Economic* perspective (top **Column.2**):

1- "*Consumer Incomes: fast rising middle class, (+ve)*": middle class fast rising in China is an important point for DeBeers to consider: if the middle class is richer they would be inclined to buy more diamonds. This is a positive *dimension* and the impact on DeBeers goal would be positive.

2- "*Costs and quality of natural, financial & human resources (+ve)*": a definite positive impact! Do you agree? If so, why? if not, why not?

3 "*Information Knowledge, (+ve)*": China is developing very fast and its technology is gaining considerable grounds, nationally and abroad, and so is its 'information knowledge'. This constitutes a short *distance*, and therefore a positive *impact*, for DeBeers move to China, from this '*Economic*' perspective of the CAGE model.

You should have by now got some clear idea as to how to proceed with the CAGE analysis. Later on, in the practice session of the project, you will have the opportunity to do **some of this kind of work by yourself in order to develop, on one side, your understanding of the principles involved** and, on the other side, the application by yourself of the CAGE framework.

Addressing all the four perspectives / dimensions of the CAGE model together will enable you to develop a helicopter view of the analysis. This is addressed next.

5. THE CAGE - FROM ALL FOUR PERSPECTIVES

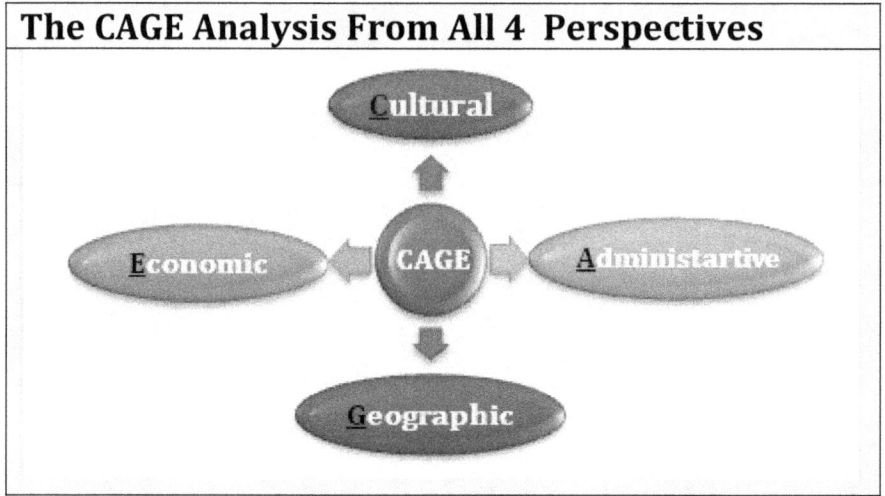

Figure.11: The CAGE, From All Four Dimensions - Context

This section pulls together all the constituent-parts of the CAGE model analysis. It actually considers the complete CAGE analysis diagram (**Figure.11**), as opposed to focusing on each perspective separately, as done before now. This will be a complete analysis from all four dimensions (Cultural, Administrative, Geographic and Economic).

So, let us remind ourselves of three key elements concerning the CAGE analysis before we start translating our visual diagram into a data format table which will cover all the elements. In a nutshell, we have looked at the trees one by one. Now we are going to look at the forest, to get an idea of what it is about this forest of the four perspectives put together.

Keep in mind that the CAGE framework is used to identify the **distance** of the organization under study: how far this is from its desirable destination. This will enable us to assess the *impact* of the *distance* from four different perspectives. We've done it one perspective at a time; now, we're going to look at them together and determine if the impact is negative or positive.

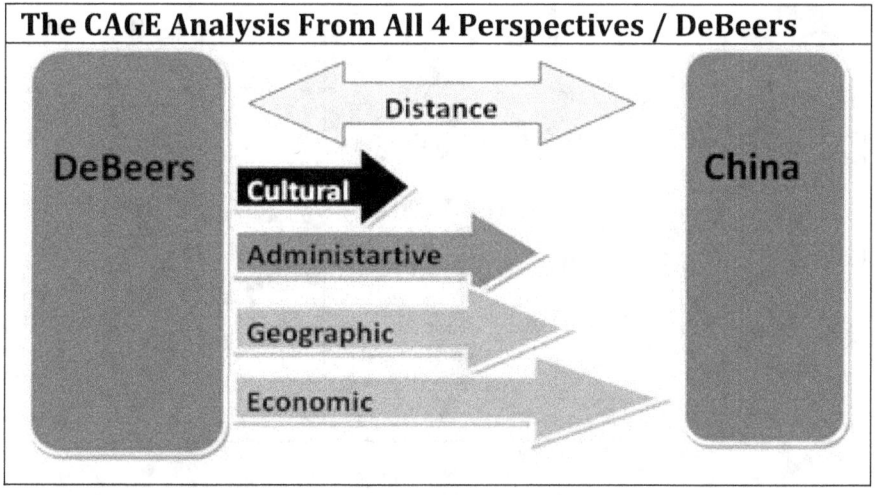

Figure.12: The CAGE, From All Four Dimensions - Study

(**Figure.12**) portrays the CAGE analysis framework complete with all four dimensions taken together. We are therefore going to try and translate this conceptual diagram into a data format, a table, which could serve well our purpose of report: report to yourself, to your boss, to a customer, see (**Table.5**).

(**Table.6**) presents the overall 'state of affaires', while each of its (**Columns.2 to .5**) addresses one of the four dimensions of the CAGE Model: Cultural, Administrative, Geographic and Economic, so as to look at them together.

Table.6: The CAGE Analysis - From All 4 Perspectives (1/2)

The CAGE Analysis, From All 4 Perspectives / DeBeers-1					
Table.1 [adapted from *(Ghemawat, P., 2004-p.1)*]: *'CAGE Framework, Why did DeBeers go to China'*					
[-ve]=negative [+ve]=positive	Cultural (Distance)	Administrative & (Political Distance)	Geographic (Distance)	Economic (Distance)
The Distance between DeBeers and China (as potential host) increases when the aspect under consideration is marked: [-ve]	*Differences in : - China's Culture from that in most Parts of the World where DeBeers operates:[-ve] - Ethnicities too, [-ve] - Religion and Social norms [-ve] *Lack Connective ethnic or social networks: [-ve]	*Shared monetary or political association, none:[-ve] *Political hostilities, none [+ve] *Legal Institutions tight and opening[+/-ve]; *financial institutions consolidating their base and improving [+ve]	*Common borders, none [-ve] *Waterway access [+ve] *Adequate transportation [+ve] *Communication Links [+ve] *Physical remoteness: far [-ve] *Climate, good [+ve]	*Consumer Incomes: fast rising middle class: [+ve] *Costs and quality of natural, financial & human resources [+ve] *Information Knowledge [+ve]

(Let's answer the following question (**Column.1**) from all four perspectives:
-*"The distance between DeBeers and China (as potential host) increases when the aspect under consideration is marked (-ve)"*

- Under the 'cultural distance'(**Column.2**): to go to China, DeBeers will have to focus on *"China's culture from that in most Parts of the world where DeBeers operate-(-ve)"*. That is a negative.

- A further look under the *cultural* distance reveals four other *'culture'* related items along (Column.2): *ethnicity, religion, social networks;* all of them are (-ve) from a *cultural* stand. This *cultural* dimension is no doubt problematic for DeBeers move: a negative *impact*.

- From an **administrative** stand (**Column.3**): we have a mix of positive and negative elements:

    - Shared monetary or political association, none (-ve)
    - Political hostilities... (+ve);
    - Legal Institutions (+ve / -ve)
    - Financial Institutions ... improving (+ve)

    However, this mixed rating appears predominantly positive; DeBeers will however need to dig deeper in the analysis of these results for further insights.

- From a **Geographic** point of view, (Column.4) reveals some positive aspects which China presents nationally and internationally:

    - Apart from the *'Common borders'* and the *'Remoteness'* aspect (*items 1 & 5*) which are *negative* and therefore constitute a negative *impact* for DeBeers, because their base is further away, in Europe,

    - The remainder of the aspects are *positive* from DeBeers point of view, under this ***Geographic*** dimension.

- Finally, the ***Economic*** dimension reveals some attractive aspects for DeBeers as far as their move to China is concerned (**Column.5**). These include:

    - "*Consumer incomes fast rising middle class, (+ve)*": probably the best point for Debeers Goal
    - "*Costs and quality of natural financial and human resources, (+ve)*": again that is here an important point.
    - "*Information knowledge, (+ve)* ": this follows on from the technology which is a Chinese forte.

We have thus addressed all four perspectives of the CAGE model, as a global analysis operation.

To empower the analysis, let's seek further insights by answering the following question: *"Does the distance affect most of the diamond industry in China?* **(Column.1, Table.7)***"*

Table.7: The CAGE Analysis - From All 4 Perspectives (2/2)

The CAGE Analysis, From All 4 Perspectives / DeBeers-2				
Table.1 [adapted from *(Ghemawat, P., 2004-p.1)*]: *'CAGE Framework, Why did DeBeers go to China'*				
[-ve]=negative [+ve]=positive	Cultural (Distance)	Administrative & (Political Distance)	Geographic (Distance)	Economic (Distance)
Does the Distance affect most the diamond industry in China?	*Not high Linguistic content [+ve] *Not related to Chinese Identity[+ve] *Not carrying country-specific quality association: [+ve}	*China Government does not view as staples, building national reputation nor as vital to national security: [+ve]	*High value-to-low weight ratio: [+ve] *Not Fragile nor perishable [+ve] but too precious [-ve] *in which communications are vital [+/-ve]	* diamond demand varies according to income: bigger purse, bigger diamond[-ve] *In diamonds labor and cost differences matter [+/-ve]

- From a ***Cultural*** point of view, three aspects are identified (**Column.2**) and all three are positive. These points include:

  - *" Linguistic content ..."*
  - *" ...Chinese identity..."*
  - *" Country specific quality association..."*

They (the three points) present therefore a short *distance* for DeBeers to "cross" for their move to China: a positive impact from these three aspects, under the *Cultural* perspective of the CAGE Model analysis. This *Culture* dimension which did not appear to be very attractive in the first part of the analysis, is now most favourable for DeBeers move to China.

- From an ***Administrative*** perspective (**Column.3**):
 - *"China's government does not view as Staples, building national reputation nor as vital to national security, +(ve)"*:

this administrative dimension is most favourable, it presents a short distance and a positive impact for DeBeers goal (to move to China)

- From a ***Geographical*** perspective (**Column.4**):
 De Beers going to China sees this first element *"high-value-to-low ration"* as positive

- The second element presents a negative and a positive impact: *(Diamonds) not fragile, nor perishable (+ve), but too precious (-ve).*

Diamonds are not fragile nor are they perishable; that's positive. But they are too precious, that's negative. This need not be discussed more as it has already been covered previously. DeBeers need to weigh the two sides of this equation.

 - *"In which communications are vital, (+ve / -ve)*:

as the element before we need to refer to the previous discussion and understand that in such 'half-way' situation DeBeers would need to delve deeper to assess how this distance can be exploited.

- From an ***Economic*** perspective (**Column.5**):
 - *"Diamond demand varies according to income: bigger purse, bigger diamond, (-ve)"*: would you agree that this aspect is negative? You could develop an argument for this being 'positive'.

- *" In diamonds labour and cost differences matter, (+ve / -ve)*: can be positive or negative at the same time, another 'half way' situation to analyse further.

This completes our CAGE analysis from the four perspectives combined, the purpose of which is to dress a global (a helicopter) view from which you can develop a full report on the situation under study. The next practice section constitutes your project whereby you get the opportunity to do your own analysis based on the CAGE model: **item by item, perspective** by perspective and then putting it all together was done up to now.

6. THE CAGE- PROJECT (PRACTICE)

This last part of this section about the CAGE framework. This time we are going to do a project. You are going to do the project. You're going to get some inspiration from the notes in the resources part (**Annex-A, Resources**). And you are going to build up your analysis, perspective by perspective, starting off by the *Cultural* (**Figure.13**).

You'll draw your diagram in this way and you look at the diamond industry in China and draw conclusions, from a *Cultural* perspective, as to why DeBeers, leaders in the diamond industry, went to China.

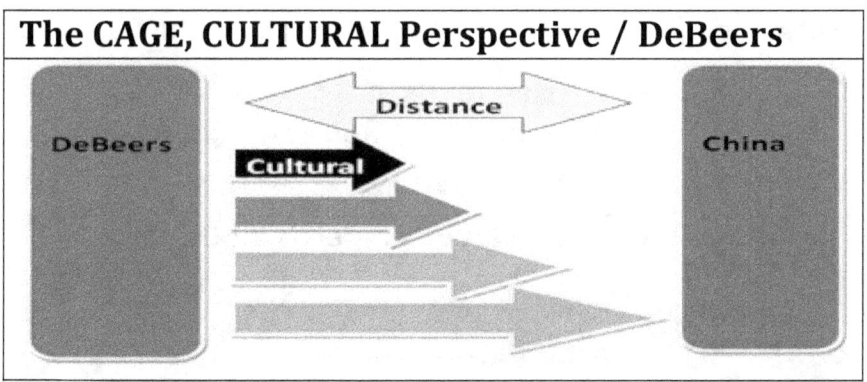

Figure.13: The CAGE, Project (Practice): 'Cultural Distance'

You have got some notes in the (**Annex-A, Resources**). Use them for ideas and inspiration about DeBeers' story, about the data source and build it up in your own way. We've done that all along this analysis, earlier on, but this time, it is going to be in your own way.

And by the way if you really want to, you could use your story as your own story at work, or your own story about a company you know, or about a situation you are familiar, a situation you want to build an analysis on.

At the end of this you will build a table just as we have done during the analysis (**Table.8**). That will be the first table of four.

Table.8: The CAGE, Project (Practice): 'Cultural' Distance'

The CAGE Project / CULTURAL Perspective / Table-1	
[Table-1a]	Cultural (Distance)

You will eventually put them together to dress the global analysis (final) table that can be used as a report.

Second perspective you are going to tackle, the *Administrative*:

In the same way, you look at the diamond industry in China from an *Administrative* point of view (**Figure.14**).

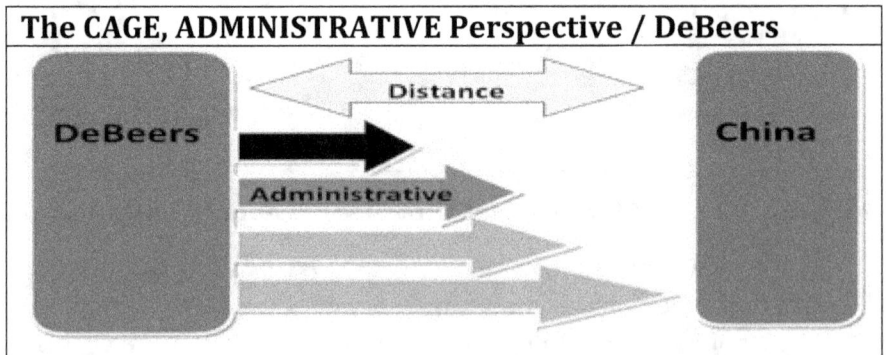

Figure.14: The CAGE, Project: 'Administrative Distance'

You read the notes in the (**Annex-A, Resources**) for ideas and inspiration and you build you a presentation of the situation in this way and you move on and take that information and tabulate it. And that's going to be your second table (**Table.9**) towards your final project.

Table.9: The CAGE, Project: *'Administrative' Distance'*

The CAGE Project / ADMINISTRATIVE Perspective / Table-2	
[Table-1b]	Administrative (Distance)

You do the same for the Geographic perspective, the third dimension (**Figure.15**):

Consult (**Annex-A, Resources**) for ideas and inspiration and build up your table.

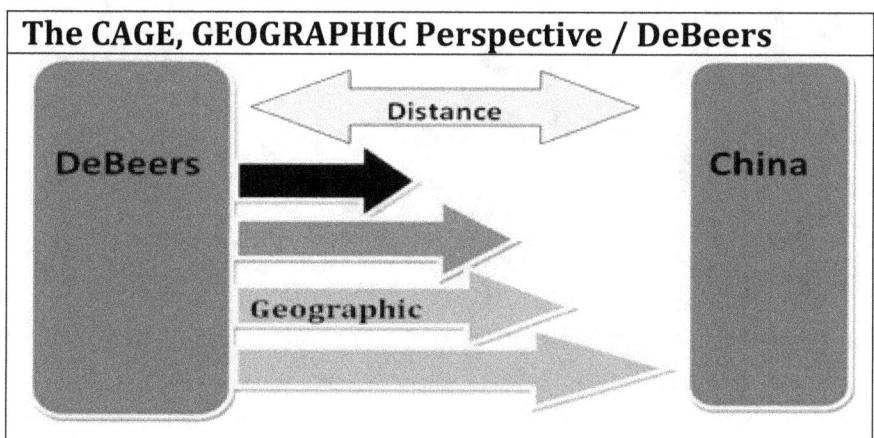

Figure.15: The CAGE, Project: 'Geographic Distance'

You build you a presentation of the situation in this way and you move on and take that information and tabulate it. And that's going to be your third table (**Table.10**) towards your final project.

Table.10: The CAGE, Project: *'Geographic' Distance'*

The CAGE Project / GEOGRAPHIC Perspective / Table-3	
[Table-1c]	Geographic (Distance)

And, you do the same thing for the Economic dimension (Figure.16).

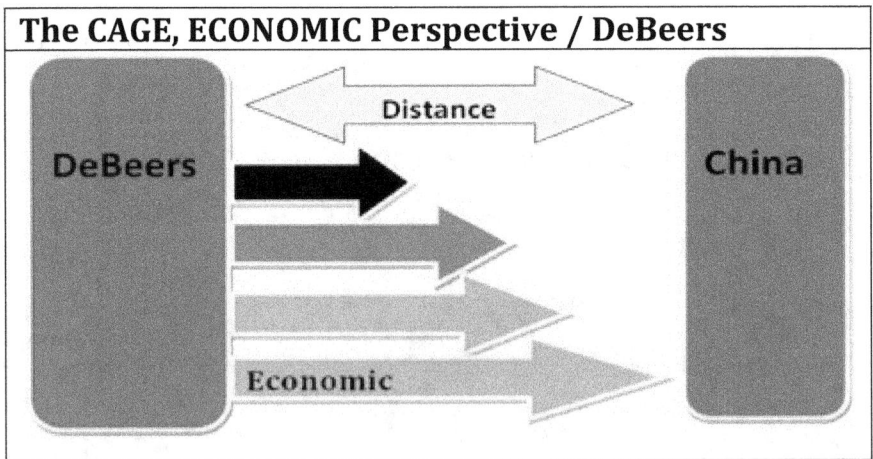

Figure.16: The CAGE, Project: 'Economic Distance'

Here you build your last table, the Economic Distance table (**Table.11**)

This then completes your four individual tables.

Table.11: The CAGE, Project: *'Economic' Distance'*

The CAGE Project / ECONOMIC Perspective / Table-4	
[Table-1d]	Economic (Distance)

You have looked at every tree I remember and now you build up your table and then you move on to the forest (**Figure.17**)

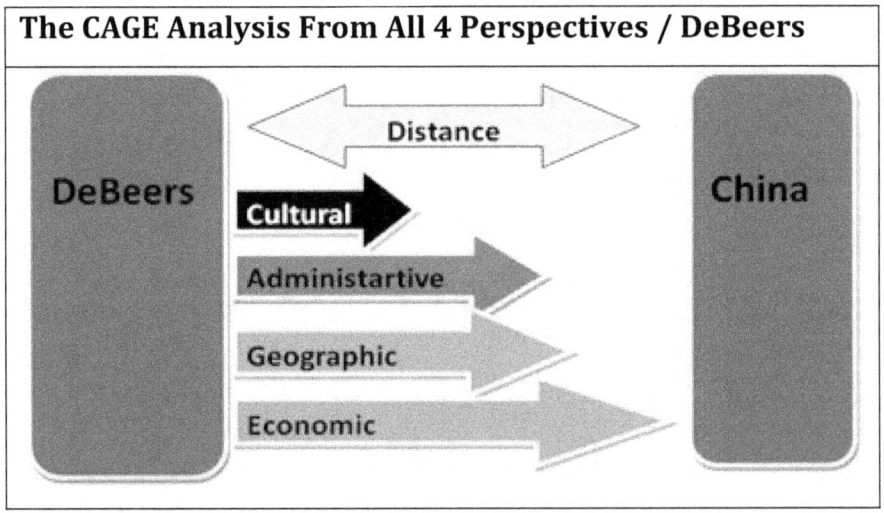

Figure.17: The CAGE, Project: 'Global Analysis'

whereby you're going to get all the info all the info culture administrative geographic economic in the table (**Table.11**) and then that's going to be the basis for your report. And also such case frame work Global Analysis constitutes a solid base for decision making.

Table.12: The CAGE, Project (Practice): *'Global' Analysis'*

The CAGE Project / From All 4 Perspectives / Table-5				
CAGE Framework Global Analysis, Base for Decision Making				
[-ve] =negative [+ve] =positive	Cultural (Distance)	Administrative (Political Distance)	Geographic (Distance)	Economic (Distance)

I wish you good luck! As I indicated earlier on, you may, if you prefer, use your own data source from somewhere else: from a situation you know, from a situation you want to tackle, from a situation you want to apply the CAGE Framework analysis to.

ANNEX - A: RESOURCES (THE CAGE)

Resource-1: CAGE Analysis, Case Study 'DeBeers'

From a strategic perspective, why did DeBeers go to China?

To develop a fuller picture as to why DeBeers went to China we shall use the **CAGE** (Cultural, Administrative, Geographic and Economic) Framework, so as to determine more objectively the distance between the two entities along these four basic dimensions as outlined by *(Ghemawat, P., 2004).* **Table.1 (Annex)** is used to depict these distances through appropriate attributes with regard to the diamond industry in China (DeBeers domain) and derive possible conclusions as to why, from a strategic perspective, DeBeers went to China.

(1)- Culture distance: (Table.1a)
Based on (**Table.1a**), the attributes of ethnicity, social networks, religion and social norms related to the China diamond market are clearly [-ve], i.e. negative: they increase the 'Cultural Distance' in DeBeers analysis of 'going to China'. The Language attribute as well, although English is most commonly used there and could be perceived as [+/-ve], i.e. neutral in the analysis. Although this overall cultural perspective is 'gloomy', the 'cultural distance' with regard to the diamond industry would be greatly reduced by the fact this industry is less affected by those cultural attributes (see lower portion of the (**Table.1**) and would not have discouraged DeBeers to go to China.

Moreover, the diamond culture in China did not offer market attraction for DeBeers: " Two decades ago in China there was no diamond acquisition culture ... hardly any Chinese brides received diamond engagement rings" reported Gareth Penny (MD of DeBeers) *[4]< www.77diamonds.com >*; and "When we started marketing on the mainland in 1993, diamonds had no emotional significance ..."- *[6]*
< articles.economictimes.indiatimes.com > said Christina Hudson (DeBeers, Marketing Director, Greater China).

(2)- Administration: (Table.1b)
The Administrative and political barriers in China have raised concern so much in terms of "market-access restrictions, high taxes, customs duties, corruption, undue government intervention in the economy " . More so with regard to some industries than others. Although as **(Column-2, Table.1b)** shows (lower portion) the Administration distance is not increased with regard to the diamonds industry [as it would have in the case of 'communications', 'security', 'natural resources' etc]. China's non existing diamonds market (as above) would have thus been perceived by DeBeers as favorable and by China as welcome: 'reduction in distance' would be hence [+ve].

"Cultural and Administrative distance produces even larger effects"- *(Ghemawat, P., 2004),* which was not the case for DeBeers.

(3)- Geography: (Table.1c)
(Table.1) shows some positive key elements with regard the Geography distance from DeBeers' perspective. Although China remoteness is a negative aspect (and no common borders that may help) waterway access, adequate transportation, good communication links, favorable climate compensate largely. What tips the balance even further (at this level) – and "reduce

the distance" - in favor of DeBeers going to China is the high value-to-low weight ratio that is associated with his diamond industry. Moreover, "DeBeers dominated the diamond industry by using the geographic advantage held by South Africa..." *[5]< www.thinkingeconomics.net>*. This geographic monopoly has collapsed and China could offer his next geographic advantage.

(4)- Economy: (Table.1d)

"DeBeers [always] used their competition advantages and resources in the most economically profitable ways" *[5]< www.thinkingeconomics.net>*. And, they want have a strong presence in developing countries, and outside USA and Europe, where market decline was showing. China became a market segment to focus on, because of its market potential, the size of its consumer base, its fast growing economy and its continuously increasing middle class. This rising affluent class constituted an attractive customer base for DeBeers, and one fundamental reason for moving to China; and "traditional economic factors, such as the country's wealth and size (GDP), still matter..."- *(Ghemawat, P., 2004)*

Although the diamond culture in China did not offer market attraction (above), but it presented DeBeers with a virgin market instead. In terms of (Kotler, P., 2006-p.350), this translates into "New users among [ALL] three groups: those who might use [its product] but do not (market-penetration strategy), those who have never used it (new-market segment strategy), or those who live elsewhere (geographical expansion strategy).

Resource-2:

CAGE Analysis, the 4 Individual Perspectives

The CULTURAL Perspective

[Table-1a] ---------------------------------- [-ve]=negative [+ve]=positive	Cultural (Distance)
The Distance between DeBeers and China (as potential host) increases when the aspect under consideration is marked: [-ve]	* **Differences in** : - China's Culture from that in most Parts of the World where DeBeers operates:[-ve] - Ethnicities too, [-ve] - Religion and Social norms [-ve] * Lack Connective ethnic or social networks: [-ve]
Does the Distance affect most the diamond industry in China?	* Not high Linguistic content [+ve] * Not related to Chinese Identity[+ve] * Not carrying country-specific quality association: [+ve}

The ADMINISTRATIVE Perspective

[Table.1b]: CAGE Analysis of " DeBeers went to China", From the 'Administrative' perspective of the CAGE Framework.	
[-ve]=negative [+ve]=positive	**Administrative & (Political Distance)**
The Distance between DeBeers and China (as potential host) increases when the aspect under consideration is marked: [-ve]	• Shared monetary or political association, none: [-ve] * Political hostilities, none [+ve] * Legal Institutions tight and opening[+/-ve]; * financial institutions consolidating their base and improving [+ve]
Does the Distance affect most the diamond industry in China?	* China Government does not view as staples, building national reputation nor as vital to national security: [+ve]

The GEOGRAPHIC Perspective

[Table-1c] -------------------------------- [-ve]=negative / +ve]=positive	Geographic (Distance)
The Distance between DeBeers and China (as potential host) increases when the aspect under consideration is marked: [-ve]	* Common borders, none [-ve] * Waterway access [+ve] * Adequate transportation [+ve] * Communication Links [+ve] * Physical remoteness: far [-ve] * Climate, good [+ve]
Does the Distance affect most the diamond industry in China?	* High value-to-low weight ratio: [+ve] * Not Fragile nor perishable [+ve] but too precious [–ve] * in which communications are vital [+/-ve]

The ECONOMIC Perspective

[Table-1d] ---------------------------------- [-ve]=negative / [+ve]=positive	Economic (Distance)
The Distance between DeBeers and China (as potential host) increases when the aspect under consideration is marked: [-ve]	* Consumer Incomes: fast rising middle class: [+ve] * Costs and quality of natural, financial & human resources [+ve] * Information Knowledge [+ve]
Does the Distance affect most the diamond industry in China?	* diamond demand varies according to income: bigger purse, bigger diamond [-ve] * In diamonds labor and cost differences matter [+ve /-ve]

The **CAGE** Framework is used to identify the ***distance of the organization*** under study (how far it is from its desired destination) and to assess ***the impact of this 'distance'***, from four different perspectives: Cultural, Administrative, Geographic and Economic. The impact, in each of these four cases, could be negative (-ve) or positive (+ve).

Resource-3: CAGE Analysis, from the 4 Perspectives1

Table.1 [adapted from *(Ghemawat, P., 2004-p.1)*]:
'CAGE Framework, Why did DeBeers go to China'

[-ve]=negative [+ve]=positive	Cultural (Distance)	Administrative & (Political Distance)	Geographic (Distance)	Economic (Distance)
The Distance between DeBeers and China (as potential host) increases when the aspect under consideration is marked: [-ve]	* Differences in: - China's Culture from that in most Parts of the World where DeBeers operates:[-ve] - Ethnicities too, [-ve] - Religion and Social norms [-ve] * Lack Connective ethnic or social networks: [-ve]	* Shared monetary or political association, none:[-ve] * Political hostilities, none [+ve] * Legal Institutions tight and opening[+/-ve]; * financial institutions consolidating their base and improving [+ve]	* Common borders, none [-ve] * Waterway access [+ve] * Adequate transportation [+ve] * Communication Links [+ve] * Physical remoteness: far [-ve] * Climate, good [+ve]	* Consumer Incomes: fast rising middle class: [+ve] * Costs and quality of natural, financial & human resources [+ve] * Information Knowledge [+ve]
Does the Distance affect most the diamond industry in China?	*Not high Linguistic content [+ve] *Not related to Chinese Identity[+ve] *Not carrying country-specific quality association: [+ve}	* China Government does not view as staples, building national reputation nor as vital to national security: [+ve]	* High value-to-low weight ratio: [+ve] * Not Fragile nor perishable [+ve] but too precious [–ve] * in which communications are vital [+/-ve]	* diamond demand varies according to income: bigger purse, bigger diamond[-ve] * In diamonds labor and cost differences matter [+/-ve]

BIBLIOGRAPHY (THE CAGE)

Internet:

[1] < http://www.telegraph.co.uk/finance/4477345/De-Beers-forms-alliance-with-LVMH.html>, accessed 1st June, 2011

[2] <http://www.jingdaily.com/en/luxury/chinas-diamond-rush-video/>>, accessed 1st June, 2011

[3] http://business.globaltimes.cn/industries/2010-01/500580.html,>, accessed 1st June, 2011

[4] <http://www.77diamonds.com/blog/diamonds-why-it%E2%80%99s-a-good-time-to-invest_981.html>, accessed 1st June, 2011

[5] <http://www.thinkingeconomics.net/ch07/s03/c7s3e1.htm>, accessed 1st June, 2011

[6] <http://articles.economictimes.indiatimes.com/2007-10-17/news/27682750_1_diamonds-david-rudlin-jewellery-trade-association>, accessed 2n June, 2011

[7] <http://www.miningweekly.com/article/chinese-diamond-market-catching-up-with-us-de-beers-2010-06-23 >, accessed 31st May, 2011

[8] **<http://online.wsj.com/public/page/news-asia-business.html>, accessed 1st June, 2011**

[9] < http://www.diamondthrills.co.uk/2011/02/looking-for-trends-in-de-beers-2010-results/>, accessed 31st May, 2011

[10] <http://www.rough-polished.com/en/exclusive/45981.html>, accessed 1st June, 2011

Books:

- Hill, T., (2000), "Operations Management, Strategic Context and Managerial Analysis": Palgrave, Hampshire, England
- Kotler, P., & Keller, K. L., (2006), *'Marketing Management'*, 12e, Prentice Hall: Pearson Education, Inc, 2006.

Publications (articles, studies, ...):

- Ghemawat, P., (2004), "Distance Still Matters, the Hard Reality of Global Expansion': The Harvard Business Review

SECTION III

"LEARN AND APPLY THE 'SMART' GOALS MODEL "

Objective:

To Master Architecture, Perspective and Application of the SMART Five Key Elements: Specifiable, Measurable, Accessible, Realistic and Time-Bound.

THE 'SMART MODEL' - INTRODUCTION

1. SMART OBJECTIVES - WHAT ARE THEY?

Figure.1: S.M.A.R.T Objectives: What Are They?

The SMART Model is often considered in the context of the Business Analysis Tools such as the PESTLE Analysis, the CAGE, the 7S Framework, etc.

Although the SMART Model is appropriate in any of the above situations, we shall deal with it here separately, but it can be called upon to complete any of the analysis above.

The question we are going to raise first is " What are the SMART Goals / Objectives?".

On the outset the SMART Model offers you a structured method to set your goals efficiently and effectively. It does provide you with an Approach to reaching your Goals, but it certainly doesn't cater for every eventuality in life.

Figure.2: S.M.A.R.T Goals, Key Elements

As such the SMART Model offers us a well focused approach on Decision Making, a credible method to help us establish and monitor our goals.

It further leads us to ensure that these goals are met. As depicted by (**Figure.2**) These goals are and should be S.M.A.R.T, that is: Specific, Measurable, Accessible /Attainable, Realistic and Time-Bound.

The SMART Goals Model depicted in (**Figure.3**) can help us enhance and improve our life (or our business) - depending on whether we set them for our life or our business. It does so by enabling us to stay on track, by helping us steer our boat to the target, to a desirable, "decided for" target.

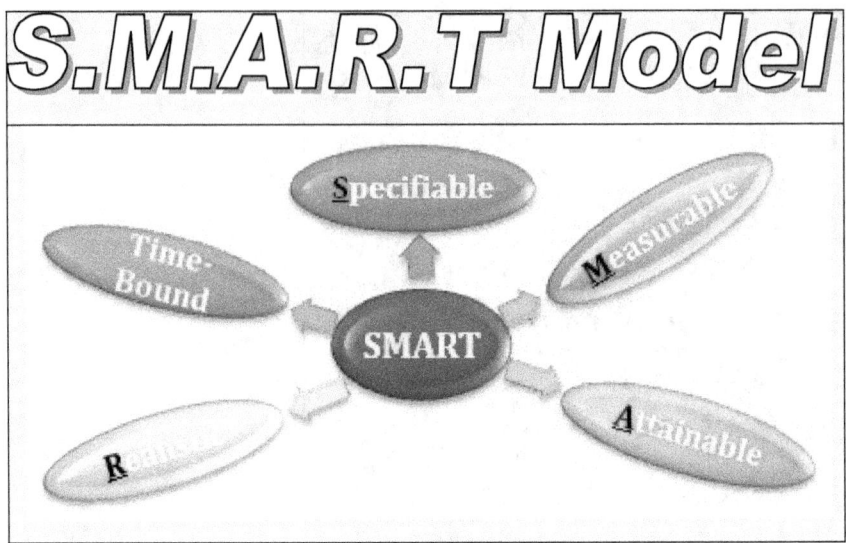

Figure.3: S.M.A.R.T Goals, the Model

2. SMART OBJECTIVES - WHAT FOR?

We continue to explore the SMART Goals, and this time we want to ask ourselves a pertinent question: "The SMART Goals, What For?"; Why do we need the SMART Goals?

Basically, the SMART Goals offer us better structuring of our goals and they can help us accomplish our tasks more thoroughly, in less time. They enable us to be more focused more productive and thus more efficient. That's: focused, productive and efficient.

The first step on the road to achievement is setting up our goals, be it in business or in personal life. Therefore, we need to set up our goals in a way that they become: Specifiable, Measurable, Accessible, Realistic and Time-Bound.

In business, Goals were found to be empowering in several key areas, categorized as follows:

- Provision of direction and guidance
- Aid of planning,
- Support in employees' inspiration and motivation, and
- Service which they facilitate in controlled performance and evaluation.

In short that's the vision behind the SMART Goals Model. As will be underlined next setting up Goals is crucial to the planning of business and personal objectives.

They are crucial to the business strategy development. They're crucial to team management, as well as to the alignment of the team members' goals with their own individual tasks and with the company's vision.

Thus, goals will help us to align the team members goals with the company's vision. Moreover, they need to be well-thought-out and credible. With that in mind, we just don't our important things haphazardly so as to get there quicker. We need to really think them over so that they become credible goals. That's why we go through this five-stages cycle of S.M.A.R.T.

Too ambitious or less challenging Goals? Either case is a recipe for failure and may impact negatively on the team members, on their stimulation drive and motivation. Too-high-set and people can't reach them or too-low-set and people will overtake them. If Goals are too ambitious people will be struggling to reach them; if they are less challenging then people will get there quicker and they will be de-motivated.

Still on the subject of what Goals need to be: we need them to be well balanced, achievable, attainable and yet challenging. They need to be clear and precise in their specification. So that's why we start off by saying "Specifiable": they need to be clear and they need to be within their specification.

A SMART Goal Model, as reflected by (**Figures.1 & 2**) gives us a clear purpose and the most likely stress free and successful outcome. Moreover, the SMART Goals mentioned therein need to conform to the SMART criteria: Specifiable, Measurable, Accessible (*), Realistic (*) and Time-Bound.

(*) **Note** that some people use the terms Assignable, Attainable, Achievable or Actionable (instead of Accessible); other talk of Relevant (instead of Realistic) goals. It is thus important at this stage to be aware of the different terminology used in the model interpretation.

Let us now look at how George T. Doran - credited with the Original SMART Model - define the acronyms of the Model "S.M.A.R.T":

- "**Specific**": that is focalise towards a specific area for improvement and be precise in what you have set yourself to achieve. That's how Doran defines "*Specific*", the first element of the Model.

- **"Measurable"**: an objective is *Measurable* means that it is quantifiable: an indicator or a progress measure of success is set out for the objective. Thus, we need to have a measure of success, we need to be able to measure our objective. If we cannot measure it, we will not know if we have attained it or not.

- **"Assignable / Attainable / Achievable/ Actionable"**: that sets the accountability by specifying who will do the task in hand, in light of the next milestone and action. It means *Assign* a goal.

   Some people would say that the goal is *assignable* if it can be assigned to somebody and we know who it is assigned to. The latter action reflects why some SMART Models emphasize the *actionable* aspect of goals while others do speak of *attainable* and *achievable*. There are some discrepancies between the terminologies that are used. But, eventually they will all be homing towards the same general idea.

- **"Relevant or Realistic"**: that tells us that the objective states what results can *realistically* be achieved through priority determination. That means we can define an objective, but it may not be *realistic*. This suggests that it has been exaggerated or it is not really *relevant* to the situation we are dealing with. So, we need to ensure *relevance* of the goals; we need to make sure that the *relevance* is respected. According to the version of the Model being used, emphasize one or the other: realistic or relevant.

- **"Time-Bound / Time Related"**: if you don't associate a *time* with a particular task you will not be able to achieve that task within a reasonable timeframe. And, when we start talking about reasonable we are in "subjective ground": what's reasonable for me may not be reasonable for you. So, to get over this ambiguity we must set a *time* to the task, a time for our objective. I should *attain* this specific objective by the end of next month: that is *Time-Bound*.

3. SMART KEY ELEMENTS - "SPECIFIC"

Figure.4: S.M.A.R.T Key Elements: Specifiable

We move on now and cover the SMART Model in some detail, starting by its first key element **"S: Specific"**- (**Figure.4**).

The "**S**" (of S.M.A.R.T) refers to "*Specific*". It has been demonstrated times and again that easy *abstract and vague* goals such as "do one's best" / "I do my best" often lead to much lower level of achievements than *specific* and challenging goals like "*increase revenue by 10 percent over a period of 12 months*".

The first is very subjective, is very vague. The second is more *specific* and with it, we would know at all times what is meant by "*increased revenue by 10 percent over a period of twelve months*". This latter goal is what we call *specific*. It is what the Model refers to through its "S" (in S.M.A.R.T). It is defined in terms of the precise results. In the above example, the result that is sought is 10 percent. It reflects clarity and, very often, supports motivation as people know exactly what to expect by such a statement of specificity.

If we go back to the statement mentioned above: " I *will do my best*". This is rather subjective and comparatively lacks definition. Often we speak of "*healthy, wealthy, happy...*": these words mean different things to different people. They are subject to the interpretation of the actor.

Making new goals more specific will make them easier to achieve. Thus if you make them less specific, that will make them harder to achieve, in general, and more difficult to measure (in terms of success), in particular. The question remains: how can you measure healthy? Or, how can you measure wealthy? or, how can you measure happy? Most likely, you cannot. So, the word "*Specific*" attempts to overcome this subjectivity and seeks to bring in a degree of success and to determine the necessary action towards our goals.

4. SMART KEY ELEMENTS - "MEASURABLE"

Figure.5: S.M.A.R.T Key Elements: Measurable

The next key element of the SMART model is identified by the letter **"M"** (for *Measurement*) - (**Figure.5**)

Measurement is king, in the spirit of Edward Deming's statement: "*what gets measured, gets managed*". In other words, if we cannot measure it, we cannot manage it, which makes a lot of sense.

Once your goal is defined and specified as outlined previously, it is crucial to have a built-in capacity to measure its success or its completion and even to monitor its progress, as will be seen later on.

Such measure will indicate for you how close you are from reaching your goal. This makes your goal (or the distance from it) measurable in some way.

What does this do for you? Such measure should help track your progress, in terms of milestones for example, or units accomplished. As such, you have specified your objective and identified a set of milestones that enable you to decide how far you are from the target. That is how many milestones you have completed. Or, how many units you have accomplished. Or, how many areas you have covered by comparison to the areas that you are expected to cover. Or, what is the number of clients served. Or, what is the number of leads that have been converted.

More importantly the key to *measuring* the goal (or the distance to it) is knowing why you are measuring and why you may need more than one measurement to gauge success. Sometimes, it is not enough to just provide one single measurement, if this will not give you the complete picture. For example, in the context of local and national, a university evaluates itself locally, nationally and even internationally. So, if you are measuring the success of this university you will be measuring it locally, nationally and internationally: you will be assessing how the university is doing in the three fields.

We will see later on how this three-key-points may be used to help set up a complete measurement of the entity that we are focusing on.

An important point to remember is that using more than one measurement to gauge success requires looking at different sources of data for each measurement style. In the university example above, for instance, we would be looking at a set of data about the university entity under study from three different perspectives (local, national, international); hence the concept of *triangulation* which applies when making three measurements.

(Figure.6) reflects a situation whereby the data comes from three sources: data-type.1, data-type.2 and data-type 3. This is our goal, regarding **'measurement'**. If applied to our university example above, data-type.1, 2, 3 would equate respectively to data 'locally', 'nationally', 'internationally'.

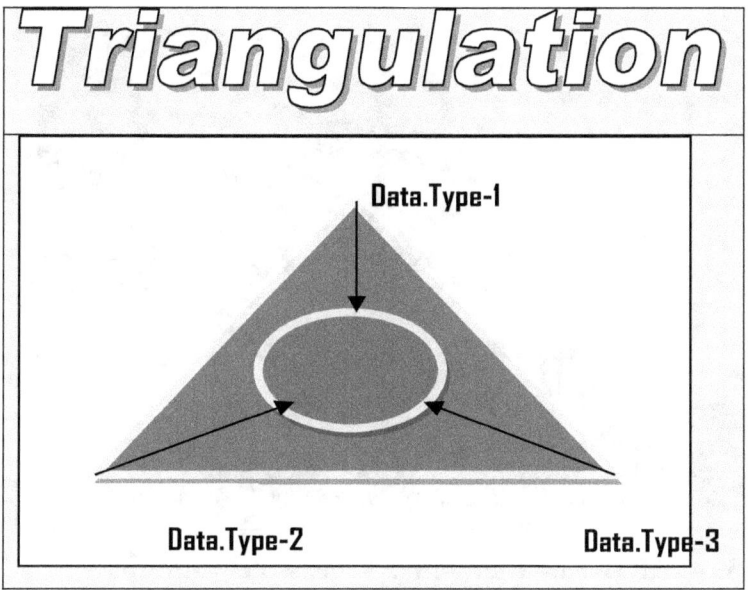

Figure.6: S.M.A.R.T Goals, Triangulation

For instance, if the university under study were to be Cambridge,

- data-type.1 (local) could be about 'Cambridge University' compared to other colleges in Cambridge town.

- data-type.2 (national) could be about Cambridge University' versus 'Oxford University', and finally

 - data-type.3 (international) could be about 'Cambridge University' versus 'Harvard University' (or MIT), for instance.

5. SMART KEY ELEMENTS - "ATTAINABLE"

Figure.7: S.M.A.R.T Key Elements: Accessible / Attainable

Let's move on now to another key element of the SMART Model, a key element somewhat ambiguous. Some would call it "Attainable", some would call it "Assignable", others would say "Accessible". There are different varieties within different Models; each one promotes the "A" (in SM<u>A</u>RT) in its own way.

Let's just get a feel of what this "A" (in SM<u>A</u>RT) could be in the different situations.

- "<u>A</u>ccountable": first of all, when talking about someone being "<u>A</u>ccountable" with regard to a given Goal, the Model expects us to make someone in charge of that Goal, someone responsible for it. That could be yourself, a team leader or any individual who would oversee the run of the project towards that Goal. "Accountable" is understood in this context.

The Goal might be your own, in which case you will be the person who is accountable for it. On the other hand, there might be somebody else in your team or the global team who is responsible for it. Although we talk about a goal being "Assignable", or "Achievable" or "Accessible", "Accountable" remains a sure way of defining the goal.

- "**A**ssignable": the SMART Model refers to a goal as "**A**ssignable", when we are expected to assign that goal to someone: someone who will be responsible for it, someone who may be responsible for the team's vision, or responsible for the implementation of the action steps towards the set goal, and for tracking the progress towards the objective.

In some forms of the SMAT Model, instead of *Assignable*, they promote the idea of the goal being *Attainable* first and *Reachable* (or *Accessible*) after. This is the *Attainability* school.

Certain Models will promote the idea of *Accountability*, making somebody *Accountable* (for the goal) first, then making it *Attainable* second. This is the *Accountability* school.

Another flavour of the SMART model, from the *Action-ability* school, drives the idea of a goal being *Actionable* first, on the basis that "a goal without action is just a dream", which is true in some way.

Another plausible version would be to look, first of all, at the *Accessibility* of the goal while keeping an eye on its *Attainability*, on its *Assign-ability* **and on all** the derivations from the "A" (in the SM**A**RT Model).

6. SMART KEY ELEMENTS - "REALISTIC"

Figure.8: S.M.A.R.T Key Elements: Realistic

Let us now consider **Relevance** ("**R**", in the SMA**R**T Model) - (**Figure.8**).

- "**R**elevant": can be used in a different ways, that is like the (A in SMART): there may be different varieties which will be pointed out along the way.

Thus far, we have covered "Specifiable", "Measurable", "Accessible", now let's look at "*Relevant*" (or "*Realistic*").

As indicated earlier, and as it is common practice, goals set for individuals or teams must be aligned with the company's vision. Thus, they must be *Relevant* to that vision. So, a company using the SMART Model may interpret and use *Relevance* in this context.

Management should ensure that employees have their goals aligned and linking back to the global team and to the wider-company, hence '*Relevant*'.

In other models it's going to be *Realistic*. We will discuss that later. In this manner, achieving goals for the employee will be a step in the direction of the wider-company goals and vice versa. Therefore, if the goals of the employees are aligned with the goals of the enterprise, then when the employees achieve their goals they would thus make one step towards the company's vision at the same time. As such, the success of one is a success for the other: a win - win situation. Employees are motivated in knowing how their work is a clear contribution to the overall picture: that is most motivating.

Although the emphasis is placed here on *Relevance*, as was pointed out earlier on, often *Realistic* appears to be used in place of *Relevant* in some SMART Model versions. Setting goals as *Realistic* remains most important. In much the same way as *Relevant* was interpreted to be an important key element of one variety of the Models, *Realistic* is also an important key element for both management and team members.

Even when the Model is based on *Relevance*, *Realistic* remains important as a secondary key element. Goals need in fact to be Realistic and Relevant. Despite the fact that the SMART Model may be biased towards one or the other, we still have to take care of both of them and bring them in so that the Model will have its full impact during the analysis of the enterprise.

7. SMART KEY ELEMENTS - "TIME-BOUND"

Figure.9: S.M.A.R.T Key Elements: Time-Bound

Let us now turn towards the last element of the SMART Model: the "T" (in S.M.A.R.**T**) - (**Figure.9**), "**Time-Bound** (or *Timely*, as some would refer to it:

    Just so that you can get an initial idea about what this key element is all about within this SMART Model, let us consider an illustrative scenario. Imagine you are onboard a plane ready to take off and the Captain of that plane makes this announcement:

> *good morning ladies and gentlemen, we will be taking off whenever we feel like it. It will take us some time to reach our destination, not sure how many, but whatever, we try to get there if we can. We have not got a flight plan at hand and hope that you don't mind it so much. Just enjoy yourselves and forget about it. Well we'll get there eventually.*

How would you feel about it? I can imagine!

That's the message that the SMART Model tries to tackle by underlining the keyword of *Time-Bound / Timely*.

Let's see this in some more official ways. The goals are structured to address the concept of time. They are set to function within a definite timescale; they are *Time-Bound*. So, the concept of time is key to the SMART Model. A definite time scale is what the Model is all about. It is what the model tries to emphasize. Goals are set against time. They are not set just haphazardly. They are set within a definite time scale, they are *Time-Bound*.

If we set a deadline for each Goal, then we would know, at all times, if we are getting close to it and if we are respecting the associated deadlines or not. Even sub-goals have times associated with them so that we are able to monitor the different milestones (and their related times) on the way towards our objective.

Moreover, time may be used as a trigger. This is to evaluate and adjust your process as required. How? We can set a specific time by which we should reach a particular milestone and when we reach that milestone we get a signal that we have arrived at that point: the time becomes the trigger to tell us that we have arrived. That is in case we cannot have a visual contact, for example.

It is important to realise that if the deadline is set wrongly, this will obviously impact on the employers or the teams in a negative way. How? this is so because if we are all under the impression (or we are all programmed) to reach our objective the twenty ninth of March in 2020 and it is that day today but we haven't reached it, that is surely not going to be quite motivating neither for the team, nor for the individual employee.

Conversely, finishing the task well ahead of the deadline makes the task of those concerned far less challenging and even de-motivating because of the abundance of time they would be left with. What will they do next since the challenge before them has been reached? Boredom settles in.

Also if the deadline is set realistically short, this could leave the team members feeling stressed. This is the case where a task that should take two weeks, for example, is expected to be completed in one week; which is most stressful, most de-motivating as the team members fail to reach their goal in the set time.

In both scenarios above the team members are disturbed. On one side, this abundance of time, this slope of nothing to do once the challenge has been reached. On the other side the team members had to struggle to get the task completed: a task that should take them two weeks they had to try and get it done in one week: a stressful situation.

The lesson to be learnt is that in both cases, if we don't manage the time, the timescale and the time frame of a task set for our staff, this will impact heavily and negatively on them; hence the importance of Time-Bound in the SMAR**T** Model.

8. SMART OBJECTIVES - "SCENARIOS / EXAMPLES"

Figure.10: S.M.A.R.T Key Elements: Scenarios / Examples

We have so far covered all the five key elements of the SMART Objectives Model: Specifiable, Measurable, Accessible, Realistic and Time-Bound. We have thus covered all the theory of the model.

We now need to do some practice through some examples (**Figure.10**), about four or five examples which are going to give you a clear indication how the goals are set to meet the SMART Goals criteria.

After that, you could practice on some real-life examples related to your work or personal situation. This will help you to get the feel of what the Model is all about and how you can apply it.

Let's look at the first example of goals that are set to meet the SMART Goals criteria. An example about "a coaching program":

- **Specifiable**: "*develop a **coaching program** to impact each of my employee's performance*". We have thus *Specified* the objective.

- **Measurable:** we now need to **Measure** / to be able to **Measure** the progress of this **coaching program** objective: "*coach each employee at least once a week*". On the basis of this statement we will set up a *Measure*: One, this will tell us that each employee has been coached; Two, this will give us an indication (a measure) which tells us that the **coaching program** has taken place once a week (coaching each employee).

- **Accessible**: "*The Human Resources Director (HRD) sets up the coaching program which is to be executed by each Head of Department*": This confirms on one side that that we have *assigned* a **coaching program** to the HRD. On the other side, the task of executing the program in favour of the teams, is *assigned* to the Heads of Departments.

Thus, we can set up a *"**Measure**"* that will enable us to tell exactly that the key element "*Measure*" is taking place and the "***Assignment***" has been met.

"*The HRD setting up the **coaching program***" applies to the first *Assignment* and "*each head of department executes the program in favour of his team*" applies to the second.

- **Realistic:** after the key element Specifiable, Measurable and Accessible comes "Realistic", the fourth element of the SMART Model.

"*Develop a coaching culture within the communication domain of the company*". Through this action, the communication domain of the company should integrate our **coaching program** within the culture of the enterprise. That makes the project realistic indeed.

- *Time-Bound:* finally to implement the "**T**" (Timely or Time-Bound of the SMART Model) we decide to *launch the program before the second quarter of this year*. Although "second quarter" may seem somewhat loose, it nevertheless identifies a deadline set up for the program. This means the timing is respected within the requirements of the SMART Model.

Let's look at a second example of goals that are set to meet the SMART Goals criteria: an example, this time, about "*online teaching with Udemy*" (a large US online teaching institution).

To Apply the SMART Model to this *online teaching with Udemy*,

- We need first of all to "***Specify***" its objective. This specification could be summarised by a statement: "*consolidate my online teaching with Udemy*". That could relate to the Instructor concerned by the project, for example. He is supposed to be already publishing courses with this institution but he needs to consolidate them.

- Applying the next key element of the SMART Model, "***Measurable***": '*launch one online course per month*'. That is the measure. If one course is launched per month, the Instructor is meeting the deadline of the objective.

The Instructor is meeting the requirement of the objective "***Accessible***". He will complete himself the different stages of each course. In this case the Model is biased more towards the ***Assignment*** (like the previous one). The Instructor would complete each stage of the courses by himself.

- ***Realistic***: "*develop rich online quality courses that lead to respectable passive income*". This is realistic. So, the Model here emphasises the *Realistic* and at the same time the *Relevance* to the Instructor's objective of online teaching with Udemy.

- Finally, the last key element of the Model, **"T" (Time-Bound / Timely**): "*implement the full program starting 1st of June next Year*". That's clear. The Instructor sets himself a deadline to meet his objective.

This second example would have given you a different perspective on the Smart Model.

The following third example is about "*a professional training website***"**: you might want to set up a website which is to promote and market your training. Let's apply the SMART Model to the case in hand:

- "***Specifiable***": specifying the objective could be "*create a professional training website for the company*". Depending on the project, this may be specified enough.

- "**Measurement**": that will be taken with regard to the achievement of the objective:

- One, will be *to acquire the Domain Name for the Website*. So we set this as a requirement, as a Measure.

- Two, *finalize the Hosting ready for next month's Contents and SEO Development*.

So, we get the Domain Name and then we Host the Website with an organization.

Specifiable, Measurable have been covered, this leads us to the third key element, next.

- *Accessible / Assignable*. "The Director to attend to (assigned) the Domain Name and Hosting; the Trainers & Marketing Manager are assigned the Contents and the Consultants are assigned the SEO of the Website".

This would require that the Director will proceed towards acquiring the Domain Name and Hosting the website. then we have a three-stages assignments (self-explanatory): three people would be responsible for the different elements of the objective in terms of **Assign-abilty**: the Director, the Trainers & Marketing Manager and the Consultant, each assigned his own task.

"*A Platform to showcase the Training Courses and improve the company image as a professional Trainer*". This is quite **Realistic**. It is also most **Relevant** to our objective of *creating a professional training and website*.

- **Timely / Time-Bound:** finally, "*the website must be ready by the end of this year*". Clearly our SMART Model has got a Time-Bound key element that is set up, a deadline of *readiness by end of the year*.

Let's look at a fourth example of goals that are set to meet the SMART Goals criteria. This time an example about "Customer Training Seminars service ".

- "**Specifiable**": the specification here is inherent in "*build a customer training seminars service in the company*". That is specified enough.

- "**Measurable**": To set up the key element "Measure" (of the SMART Model) for our training objective: '*we develop the training facilities and six core Training Seminars and Train three Trainers, each phase in one quarter (of the year)*'. These will be the milestones that we need to reach and measure on the way to our "objective". This gives us an indication how far we are from our goal of "*setting up a training seminars service*".

- One, '*develop the **training facilities**'*; we can set up a trigger here, if we want to, a 'time trigger'.

- Two, '*set up six core **training seminars**'*, another measure.

- Three, '***train three trainers***', another measure.

Moreover, we plan *each phase in one quarter of the year*, another measure. So, at each quarter, we check our milestones and

175

ensure that the appropriate action has been taken towards the achievement of the objective.

- **"Assignable"**: '*the Training Manager is expected to design the Training Seminars'*, this is one "*Assignment*". The second "*Assignment*" is for him to '*Train the Trainers*', with the collaboration of the R&D team. The Training Manager is thus *Assigned* two tasks and shares the latter with the R&D team.

- **"Realistic"** "*create a training capacity and a professional training culture within the training department of the company*". That's "***Realistic***" and "***Relevant***" to our objective.

- **"Time-Bound / Timely"**: "*training facilities ready by fourth quarter of 2019*"; we have a time scale defined here. That is to get our training facility ready by the fourth quarter of the year 2019. Another timescale is set for our '*Training Team to be ready by end of first quarter 2020*'. And, a third timescale related to the '*core training courses set to be ready by second quarter of 2020*'. We have thus set up a time for each of the tasks that need to be carried out so that we reach our objective of "*building customer training seminars service*".

Evidently, applying the SMART Model along those bases enables us to clearly define the task (specifying it), limiting in time, setting up measures for it (and its milestones). It stands to reason how useful it is for any project, how useful it is for the analysis of every situation. This will help you to get your facts clear on the task at hand by applying the SMART Model.

You can now go and take an example from your life situation or your work situation and try to apply the SMART Model to it and implement it in this manner. This will help you to make the SMART Model a tool within your capacity part of your competencies.

9. SMART OBJECTIVES - CONCLUSION

Figure.11: S.M.A.R.T Goals: Conclusion

In this section, which we call the **"Conclusions"** section (**Figure.11**), we shall emphasize some of the key elements that we have learnt about the SMART Model.

In the latter part, we have studied a set of four examples and through each example we have emphasized the attributes of the appropriate key element:

- how we can put it into an application,

- how we can specify an objective,

- how we can set up measures for it,

- how we can define that it is Accessible or Assignable,

- how we are assigning tasks that are associated with the objective within the SMART Model, how they are Assigned and whom they are Assigned to.

Let us underline at this stage some of the key concepts that we would like to put into our long term memory.

 - First of all, we said that the SMART goals offer us a structured method to set our goals efficiently and effectively.

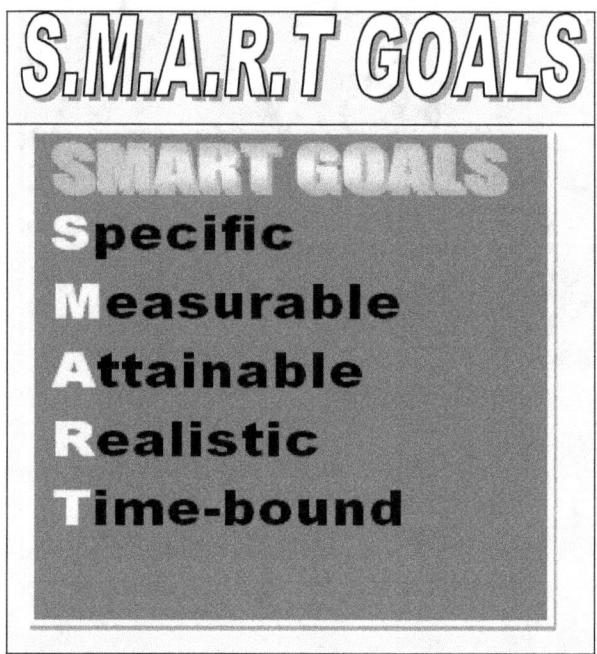

Figure.12: S.M.A.R.T Objectives: Key elements

 - Then we have emphasized that it is a tool which is well focused on Decision Making. Remember this Decision Making concept that is very important throughout our analysis.

 - The final point of the analysis is to make Decisions very often.

Moreover, we want to build a credible method that is going to help us establish and monitor our goals. All this leads us to ensure that these goals are within the SMART Model, the key elements of which are: Specific, Measurable, Attainable, Realistic and Timing-Bound (**Figure.12**)

We went through these items in greater details and looked at a set of real life examples / scenarios about each one of those, to empower practice.

(**Figure.13**) depicts a visual representation of the SMART Model with the SMART concept at the centre and the key elements around it.

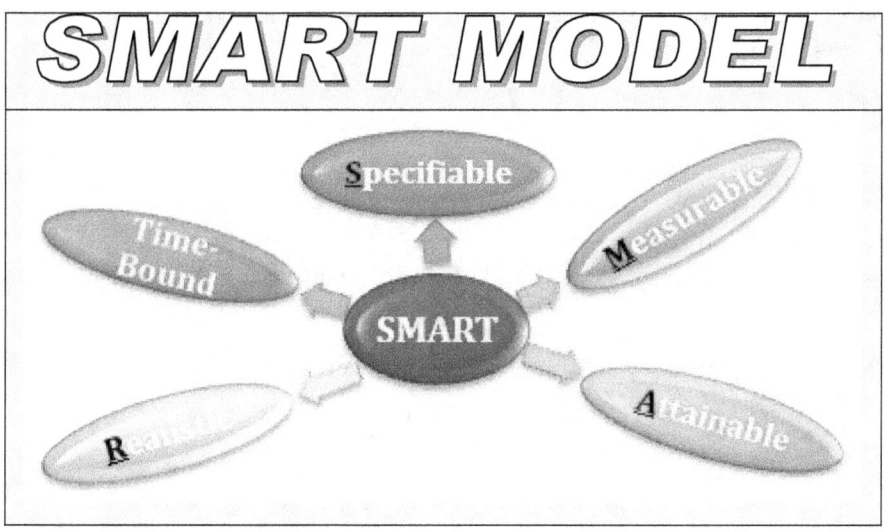

Figure.13: S.M.A.R.T Objectives: The Model

We have learnt that the SMART Goals approach can help us enhance and improve our life or our business whichever the case may be. How? By staying on target, so goals need to be well-thought-out and credible.

They must not be too ambitious or less challenging. We underlined that in both cases they would impact negatively on the team members' simulation drive and motivation. If they are too ambitions, we said that they would be inhibiting for the team, out of bounds and hard to get to. If they were less challenging, participants would not have much to strive for; they will not be stretching enough for the team members.

The goals need to be well balanced. They need to be achievable, attainable, yet challenging. Over and above being clear and precise in its specification a SMART Goal Model seeks a clear purpose and a most likely stress free and successful outcome.

Because of this balance that it provides, because of this structure, because of this guidance by the model towards our objective, then the working situation, through it, is going to be less stressful.

10. SMART OBJECTIVES - PSYCHOLOG: THE YALE STORY

Figure.14: S.M.A.R.T Model: Psychology - Yale University

This section is going to be somewhat special. It underlines the psychological benefits of the SMART Objective Model - (**Figure.14**). It is entitled the "Yale University story".

Apparently, there are some research that have been carried out at Yale University and which were quite revealing with relation to SMART Goals. Let's look them.

The story is unconfirmed. It dates back to 1953. Researchers carried out a survey within Graduates. The objective was to assess the percentage of those that had specific written goals for their future. They constituted three percent (3%). The survey was re-run some 20 years later on those same Graduates. What did they find out?

They found out that the three percent (3%) with the specific written goals where in fact richer than the remaining ninety percent (97%) combined.

This is not so surprising if you accept that that when you know where you are going you will have more chances of getting there.

This unconfirmed story remains an impactful one, told by many motivational speakers over the years. What's the message behind it?

The message is to underline the fact that Goal Setting is directly related to success in some way. From experience that one has acquired over the many years, I can vouch for that.

This may lead to different interpretations but a more plausible one appears to be that if we focus positively on what we want this will eventually trigger it into being.

I remember during one sales seminar in Oxford we were told that if you want a Rolls-Royce, just go and try a Rolls-Royce. Get closer to that objective. That strong wish may surprisingly become an objective and possibly a reality. Some associate this with *'universal consciousness'*, others talk of *'awareness in action'*. Whatever you call it - universal consciousness, or awareness in action - there is some truth in the matter. There is some truth behind it. We have all experienced it in one form or another.

Awareness in action implies that the more we become conscious of our goal the more our brain leads us towards it: awareness in action. This, in a way, completes the SMART Objective Model.

The SMART Objective Model is about setting it up; but we need to believe in it, in some way. And, that's where 'awareness and action' comes in. It implies that the more we become conscious of our goal the more our brain leads us to it.

An example to illustrate this is to set yourself a goal to focus your attention on the lorries passing by as you go for your daily walk, your daily walk to work, for example. If you set yourself such goal *'to focus your attention on the lorries passing by'*, some psychological aspect is going to take place. There is a strong tendency that **you will see many more lorries** than what you usually see without this goal in mind.

How do you explain this phenomena? Keep in mind that all things are explained, not all things are scientific facts. But some are psychologically based. The Yale story may not be a real one, as there is no confirmation of such a study around but it **remains an impactful story, told over the years since 1953 by various motivational speakers.**

11. SMART OBJECTIVES - PROJECT: HANDS-ON PRACTICE

Figure.15: S.M.A.R.T Objectives: Project

Let's have some hands-on practice: a practice exercise session, a mini project (**Figure.15**).

We have covered, thus far, the SMART Model with all its key elements (S,M,A,R,T) and some psychological perspective associated with it and underlining how useful it can be for you.

Let us now do some work, some practical work which you can attempt on your own to make the inherent powers of the model part of your own skills.

To that effect, identify two real life personal objectives that you want to set yourself in your personal life. We all have objectives in our personal life. So choose two that are very important for you and do the following work on them.

Also, identify two real-life work / business related objectives, which you want to set yourself at work. We all have got such objectives that we want to achieve, we want to reach at work.

In each of the above two situations, attempt to apply the SMART Objectives Model in full. Bear in mind the four examples /scenarios which we have covered. Do it along those lines and use the SMART Objective Model in full, through it five key elements (S.M.A.R.T).

The idea is first to learn the application of the Model and your guides, to that effect, are the four examples which we have covered.

- First, take your two personal goals and go in along the same lines of the four examples (covered) and try and apply the SMART Model Objectives and see how you can actually master it.

- Secondly, see if by doing so the model has helped you to perceive and get closer to your objective in each case. In other words, see if by applying the SMART Model to your objective this is bringing you even closer to your objective. That makes your objective clearer. That brings in more focus on your objective (c.f. the Psychological effect).

You may provide me with some feedback through Linkedin, or through my Website, if you wish to do so:

- Linkedin: https://www.linkedin.com/in/abdelali-bouzid-39091823/

- Website: www.ab-consulting-online.com

A NOTE FROM THE AUTHOR

Thank you very much for having taken the time to read:

' The PESTLE Model & The CAGE Framework: Business Analysis Tools'

If you found it interesting please take a moment to leave a review at your online convenient retailer such as Amazon UK or Amazon USA.

As an appreciated reader, your are most welcome to contact me via my website { *http://www.ab-consulting-online.com*}, to sign up for my newsletter and be notified of new releases and special offers, to read my blog, or join me / connect with me on different social networking platforms.

Abdelali BOUZID

LINKS TO THE AUTHOR @ SOCIAL & PROFESSIONAL PLATFORMS

You may reach me here:

Linkedin: *https://www.linkedin.com/in/abdelali-bouzid-39091823/*

Twitter: *https://www.twitter.com/@sonsalab*

Facebook: *https://www.facebook.com/abdelali.bouzid.3*

My Author Page: *http://amzn.to/1U2qePT*

ONLINE COURSES BY THE AUTHOR ON THE SUBJECT

The Courses below complement and empower the Topic of this Book, *"Business Analysis & Tools"*, if you enjoy quality digital content, audio and interactive online courses led by a Professional Instructor.

Over 4900 Students from about 110 Countries follow these Courses; If you want to join them:
http://ab-consulting-online.com/ur-online-courses/

Course-1:
Problem Solving & Decision Making: Tools, Techniques &Method":

{http://ab-consulting-online.com/ur-online-courses/}

Course-2
Business Analysis Tools: Apply SMART, PESTLE, CAGE, 7S, Porter's-5Forces

{http://ab-consulting-online.com/ur-online-courses/}

Course-3
Learn & Apply the Multi-Criteria Business Analysis Tool

{http://ab-consulting-online.com/ur-online-courses/}

Course-4
Learn & Apply the Business Analysis Tools: 7S & CAGE

{http://ab-consulting-online.com/ur-online-courses/}

Course-5
Learn & Apply the CAGE - Business Analysis Tool

{http://ab-consulting-online.com/ur-online-courses/}

Course-6
Learn & Apply the S.M.A.R.T Model to Business Objectives

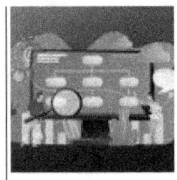

{http://ab-consulting-online.com/ur-online-courses/}

Course-7
Learn & Apply the P.E.S.T.L.E Business Analysis Tool

{http://ab-consulting-online.com/ur-online-courses/}

The PESTLE, The CAGE & The SMART Models: Business Analysis Tools

OTHER BOOKS BY THE AUTHOR

http://amzn.to/1U2qePT

'Organizational Behavior: Business Analysis through a Case Study', **Available at:** http://amzn.to/1V08IuL	
'Marketing Management: Business Analysis and Planning from a Marketing Perspective' **Available At:** http://Amzn.To/1w1ckyd	
'International Business Management Analysis: Strategy, Partnership, Investment, Benefits &Global Brands and Supply Chain. **Available At:** http://amzn.to/1LGHiaO	
Learn & Apply Business Analysis Tools: 7s Framework, Swot And Balanced Scorecard: to Assess a Small Business - Print & Kindle **Available At:** https://www.amazon.co.uk/dp/B072N9PSWG	
'Applying Business Analysis Tools: To Assess A Small Business', **Available At:** http://Amzn.To/1m9cbpx	
'The 7s Model & The Cage Framework: Business Analysis Tools' **Available at:** https://www.amazon.co.uk/dp/B085T8SXP4	
'The Pestle Business Analysis Tool: To Learn & Apply To Your Business' **Available At:** https://www.amazon.co.uk/dp/B085RB329Z	

'Business Analysis Tools: *The CAGE Framework Applied* <u>Available at:</u> https://www.amazon.co.uk/dp/B085MN1QHV	
'Business Analysis Tools: *The Multi-Criteria analysis:* *To Study Your Business* <u>Available At:</u> https://www.amazon.co.uk/dp/B085NBNLYF	
Business Analysis Tool-Kit & its Application: *7S Framework, SWOT & Balanced Scorecard* <u>Available At:</u> https://www.amazon.co.uk/dp/B084KNRXRVWG	
Learn & Apply Business Analysis Tools: *7s Framework, Swot And Balanced Scorecard:* *to Assess a Small Business - Print & Kindle* <u>Available At:</u> https://www.amazon.co.uk/dp/B072N9PSWG	

Abdelali BOUZID

A WHOLE SERIES OF EBOOKS AND THEIR ACCOMPANYING ONLINE COURSES HAVE BEEN PUBLISHED BY THE AUTHOR TO OFFER THE FOLLOWER A COMPREHENSIVE BUSINESS ANALYSIS JOURNEY FROM DIFFERENT PERSPECTIVES,

Check them out here:
1- *http://ab-consulting-online.com/ur-kindle-books/*
2- *http://ab-consulting-online.com/ur-online-courses/*

www.ingramcontent.com/pod-product-compliance
Lightning Source LLC
Chambersburg PA
CBHW052352220526
45465CB00003BA/1070